ESCAPED
★ WITH ★
HONOR

ESCAPED
★ WITH ★
HONOR

A TRUE STORY OF A KOREAN WAR POW/MIA

CHARLES LAYTON
GEORGIANN COONS ★ TAMMY ELMORE

WinePressPublishing
Great Books, Defined.

WinePress Publishing is honored to present this title in partnership with the author. The views expressed or implied in this work are those of the author. WinePress provides our imprint seal representing design excellence, creative content and high quality production. To learn more about Responsible Publishing™ visit www.winepresspublishing.com.

Unless otherwise noted, all Scriptures are taken from the *Holy Bible, New International Version®, NIV®*. Copyright © 1973, 1978, 1984 by Biblica, Inc.™ Used by permission of Zondervan. All rights reserved worldwide. www.zondervan.com

Scripture references marked KJV are taken from the *King James Version* of the Bible.

Scripture references marked NASB are taken from the *New American Standard Bible*, © 1960, 1963, 1968, 1971, 1972, 1973, 1975, 1977, 1995 by The Lockman Foundation. Used by permission.

ISBN 13: 978-1-4141-2540-4
ISBN 10: 1-4141-2540-2
Library of Congress Catalog Card Number: 2012922699

This book is dedicated to all service personnel who did not make it home and to all soldiers who served without family support.

The men and women who were held as prisoners of war paid an enormous price for our freedom. Many of them went missing in action, and their fate has never been resolved. Many were lost in the chaos of battle, and it is not known whether they perished or survived. Americans held captive were cruelly stripped of their freedoms, treated brutally, and used as pawns. They fought lonely battles against despair and the ultimate fear of being forgotten.

The Ranger Creed states, "Never shall I fail my comrades. I will keep myself mentally alert, physically strong and morally straight, and I will shoulder more than my share of the task whatever it may be, one hundred percent and then some."

CONTENTS

ACKNOWLEDGMENTS

I WANT TO thank everyone who encouraged me to tell my story, those who helped bring this story to fruition and those who prayed for me throughout this process. The writing, rewriting, editing, and reediting process has taken over two years and hundreds of hours. I am grateful for the dedication of time and talent given by Georgiann and Tammy.

A special thanks to my friend, Gary Leman, who shared a copy of John Stott's *Basic Christianity* with me. To paraphrase Dr. Stott, I will commit myself "heart and mind, soul and will, home and life, personally and unreservedly to Jesus Christ." I will humble myself before Him and take my place as a loyal member of the Church and responsible citizen in my community.

FREE AT LAST

I stand to sing the old-time hymn
And read each verse with care:
"I Love to Tell the Story"
Is a feeling I now share.

How long I held my story close,
How long it scarred my soul!
The guilt, despair and pain I held
Were outside my control.

Yet through some miracle of time,
Of place and friends and heart,
I set my story free at last,
Each raw and painful part.

This is my theme and driving goal:
To tell my story well;
To share with others truth and hope;
To ease their pangs and hell.

Too many brothers now are gone—
Tales etched on silent stone.
Their agonies of war and grief
Are sealed in mind and bone.

A story saves their memory,
Their passions, name and face—
Sacrifice stored on page and book
That death cannot erase.

The stories of our Savior
Were shared to set us free;
Freedom brings release and peace,
True Heaven yet to be.

Now tell your story proudly
Without despair or shame,
And live a life of joy and thanks
In the glory of His name.

INTRODUCTION

EVERY SOLDIER HAS a story, and every story is unique. Some soldiers' stories are told again and again, handed down through generations, shared in great novels, and made into blockbuster movies. Other stories are silent, held in the mind and heart of a soldier, never to be shared.

My story was untold for more than sixty years. While I am proud of my service to my country, I buried the trauma of my experience in the Korean War deep in my heart and mind. The pain associated with my capture, torture, and escape—both physical and emotional—was a terrible burden that I chose never to share. Why would I want someone else to share that pain? I didn't want anyone to have pity on me or feel sorry for me. I had decided to put my past behind me and move forward.

However, sixty years later, friends encouraged me to tell my story. They had enjoyed hearing my tales of horses, movie stars, and farm life, and they thought others might benefit from hearing about my experiences. At first I was hesitant, but I eventually realized that if one person could find hope through reading my story, it would be worth it. If one person could rise up and meet the challenges in his or her life after reading my challenges, it would be worth it. If just one fellow veteran could find a little peace in his or her heart after reading the peace I now have in mine, it would be worth it.

My story is based solely on my memory, and what follows are the events as I have been able to piece them together. I wish I could offer proof of the details you are about to read, but unfortunately the only documentation I had about the history of my service was a DD214 (Certificate of Release or Discharge from Active Duty), which is given to all servicepersons with their discharge papers. This certificate records all of a soldier's activity, including his or her combat service, awards, rank, and training.

Unfortunately, my DD214 was destroyed in a flood, and the official copy—held by the National Personnel Records Center in St. Louis, Missouri—was lost in a fire on July 12, 1973. The reproduced letter appears at the end of this book. Between sixteen and eighteen million official military personnel files were lost during this disaster—representing 80 percent of the records of army personnel who were discharged from 1912 to 1960—and no duplicate copies were ever maintained or microfilm copies produced. Therefore, the only fact I can offer as to the truth and accuracy of these Korean War stories is my word. I am a man of my word, and if these stories were not true, I would not share them with you.

PROLOGUE
THE BLIND MARE

I HEARD THE whistle of the bamboo rod as it cut through the air and then felt its sting against my skin. Again and again the North Korean guard brought the bamboo down on my cold, bare feet with all his strength. Ten … fifteen … twenty … twenty-five lashes. I might have cried out, but the pain of the beating took my breath away.

When the guard finished, he tossed me back into the darkness of the stinking "hooch." One of my fellow prisoners must have put my filthy socks back on my feet and tied up my boots, for I could feel their weight when I woke from my pain-induced sleep. I could also still feel the indentation of the bamboo rod.

For seventeen weeks, I and the thirty-six other captives endured beatings, starvation, and other tortures. For seventeen weeks we struggled to survive in that mud hut somewhere in enemy territory. For seventeen weeks we tried to sleep on the cold dirt floor, huddling together to try to gain some bit of warmth in the frigid Korean winter. For seventeen weeks I tried to keep my sanity not only by focusing on our future escape but also by allowing my mind to travel back to a happier time. My thoughts often dwelt on a blind mare I had befriended when I was nineteen.

Back then, I lived on my own in a small rented room and worked at Whitney Stables, home to some of the finest American Saddlebred horses. I walked a mile from the bus stop to the stable, but it was a walk on sunshine.

I noticed the blind mare during my first morning of work. She had been put out into the thirty-acre pasture early that morning, and the scene I beheld was better than any masterpiece. The mare was a beautiful creature with a classic long, arched neck. She had a refined face, a level back, and fine, straight legs, which were highly valued in her breed. She was a legend on the farm, as she dropped an outstanding foal every year. But she seemed skittish and lonely, so I made it my business to become her friend.

"Mare, mare," I called out as I climbed over the white three-rail fence. I said this loud enough for her to hear, but quiet enough not to scare her. I saw her prick up her ears and turn toward me. I continued to call and nicker, and ever so tentatively she walked toward the sound of my voice. When she was finally at my side, I gently stroked her neck, all the while cooing softly to her.

"Okay, girl, we're ready to go," I murmured. I walked slowly toward the other side of the pasture. In moments her gait flattened out, and she walked with more confidence. She finally laid her head on my shoulder.

We took a shortcut to the barn. When we arrived, I went in and broke off a special flake of hay for her, hoping she understood this offering of friendship. She took it from me.

Each day when I arrived at the pasture on my way to the barns, I would see the mare standing there. She was always in a different place and alone. I called out and approached her the same way every day. As the weeks passed she became more comfortable with me, but she never sensed my arrival. I would have to call or whistle for her, and she would come to me.

I treasured those pleasant minutes in good company. Now, in this hooch, the memory of that mare brought me a small bit of hope. We were a skittish and frightened crew, but with persistence I had gained the confidence of the men. With patience, we could plan and execute an escape. Deep within my heart, I heard the same sort of gentle calling I had offered to the mare: *Come, come.*

CHAPTER 1

BELONGING

W HEN I WAS a baby, I crawled out of my house and ended up on a busy street corner. A German Shepherd named Zelda stood over me and protected me from the traffic until an adult came to rescue me.

This is the only story I know from my early childhood. I don't know who owned the dog, how I got into the street, or why this is the only story I can remember my parents telling about my early years. I have no baby pictures, no happy family stories, and no beautiful memories. I do know I was born in St. Louis, Missouri, on November 6, 1928, and I was the second child in my family. My sister, Lee Ann, was born eighteen months before me. I know I must have been fed, diapered, and cared for in the usual ways, but I also know I was an unwanted burden to my parents.

In November 1928, the Great Depression was looming its ugly head over the United States, and an extra mouth to feed was certainly not seen as a blessing. In an effort to survive, in 1931 my parents relocated our family to Frankfort, Indiana, where my uncle was the county sheriff. We moved into the top floor of a two-story house. One day while I was playing at home, I looked through the heating register and saw another kid looking up at me. So I spit on that kid. Unfortunately, that kid was my sister, Lee Ann. I can assure you I never spit again, as my backside caught fire from the spanking I received from my father. However, this didn't stop my pranks.

I remember making friends with another little boy named Bobby, who was often my "partner in crime." One of our favorite pranks was to tie a string to the handles of one of my mother's empty purses and strategically place it in the middle of the street. Bobby and I would rush back to our hiding place behind a bush and await the fun.

At some point, a car would come "whizzing" by (at about fifteen miles per hour). The driver would see the purse and stop to investigate. We'd pull it quickly back with the string, and then run like crazy when we saw the surprised look on the driver's face. We laughed and laughed. We thought ourselves to be vicious, hardcore pranksters for small boys of five years.

I have many happy memories from the short time we lived in Frankfort. The hills and valleys of rural Indiana were a world of adventure for a little boy, and I spent many happy hours exploring, scheming, and pretending. No one cared how far I wandered or how long I was gone. And, no one seemed particularly happy to see me when I arrived home after one of my exciting days of adventure. No one, that is, except for Helen.

Helen was a friend of my parents, though I don't recall just how they came to know one another. I do know Helen was the first nurturing adult I had ever encountered. She was a big, roly-poly woman, and her heart was the biggest part of her. She was single and had no children. She treated me as if I were her own son, and I loved her as a mother. Helen was a bright light of joy in my early life, and one whom I came to depend on as I grew older.

My parents opened a dry-cleaning business, but as the economy grew worse, it failed. People just didn't spend their precious pennies on dry cleaning. Like others who were trying to get through the Great Depression, my parents believed their only hope of survival was in the big city. So, in 1934, they moved us to Chicago. I don't know if my dad was out of work for long, but luckily he found a position with the Dr. Scholl Foot Comfort

Company. He managed the company store in downtown Chicago.

Although I missed the beauty and freedom of the Indiana countryside, Chicago was an awesome sight for a six-year-old boy. Again, I was left to my own devices. I don't remember my parents setting boundaries, making rules, or enforcing any type of curfew. I was free to roam the city and came and went as I pleased.

Many people have found it shocking that such a small boy would be free to roam about Chicago. In fact, I have sometimes found it hard to believe myself. Who knows what sort of tragedy might have befallen? For me, however, it was just another sort of adventure, and when I left the apartment each day I found excitement on the streets.

One particularly happy memory is my morning rendezvous with the horses that pulled the milk wagons from one building to the next. I came to know the horses by name, and as the milkman jumped from the wagon and made his deliveries, I would talk with them, scratch their sides, and enjoy their company. I followed the wagon for blocks just for the chance to spend time with the horses. Every once in a while as I trailed after them, I would come upon a tiny patch of grass, which reminded me of the beauty of the country life.

Our family lived on the South Side of Chicago. When I was five years old and entered the first grade in 1934, I went to Wadsworth Grammar School, which was about a mile from our apartment. There was no bus service, so I had to run to school and, at lunchtime, run back home. The school didn't have a lunchroom and the teachers also left and closed the building at noon. After lunch, I ran back to school and then home again at the end of the day—four miles of running every day.

One especially cold day when I was coming home for lunch, I fell on the ice. Someone had dropped a glass milk bottle on the sidewalk, and when I fell, the bottle cut my leg and left a deep gash. Today, a child with such a wound would be rushed to the hospital, or at least to the nearest doctor, but no one attended to me. My parents had become Christian Scientists by this time and had fully embraced the concept that illness and injury were "false realities." Taking me to a doctor to have my wound sewn up would have been an affront to their beliefs.

Of course, at the time I didn't understand this. The parents of other kids I knew took them to the doctor when they were sick or injured, so why not me? Some years later I asked my parents why they still went to the dentist and eye doctor if they didn't believe in physicians. They explained their personal faith wasn't yet strong enough for them to overcome deteriorating eyesight or tooth decay.

The only care I received for my injured leg was when my father came home in the evening and changed my oozing, smelly bandage. He didn't seem to do this out of love; it was just another household chore he completed with a sort of resigned indifference. Though I longed to hear a few comforting, loving words from him, he didn't speak to me as he went about his work.

I never questioned my parents' religious philosophies, but I did begin to blame myself for the accident. *If only I hadn't been running—if I had been more careful—this wouldn't have happened. I should have seen that piece of glass. My injury did nothing but add more work to my parents' days.*

I couldn't walk, so I was forced to stay in my bed for weeks while the injury healed. The longer I stayed in bed, the more I thought … and the more I thought, the more confused I became. I dreaded those forty-five minutes my father spent changing the bandages each evening, because I knew I was disrupting the evening meal and all my parents' plans in the home. I was a bother to them. No one ever asked how I was feeling or seemed to care about my healing.

I am thankful the gash didn't become infected or gangrenous, and I feel lucky to have survived childhood without the aid of the medical community. Although I never completely understood the depth or intensity of my parents' faith (they never forced me to take an active part in their church activities), I do know the principles they chose to live by would greatly affect me in the coming years.

Looking back, it may seem odd that it was my father, not my mother, who cleaned my wound each evening. Knowing my mother, I am sure she "ordered" my father to do this unpleasant chore. My mother wore the pants in our family, but she was a moody woman. If she didn't get her way, she sulked, pouted, and left the apartment in a huff, not telling anyone where she was going or when she would return.

As a little boy, this frightened me. I didn't completely know how a mother acted in a typical family, but I was certain the way my mother behaved was far from it. Despite the lack of affection, she was still my mom, and I looked to her for some peace and calm. When she disappeared for hours, I was afraid that she would never return.

When I attended grammar school and then high school in the 1930s and '40s, the school year ran from Labor Day to Memorial Day, and kids became anxious and "squirmy" in May, anticipating the fun and freedom they would have all summer. But when the school year ended my first year of school, my parents shipped me off to a farm in southern Illinois. At the time I was just six years old, I was frightened, and I didn't know what to expect. I didn't feel as if I belonged at home, but in many ways I considered this separation from the family as a punishment. Certainly, it was a clear indicator that my parents didn't want me around. Of course, with me away for the summer, my parents had one less person to support for four months.

For five straight years, the morning after school ended, my mother put me on that southbound bus. I sat up front with the bus driver and watched the passengers board. As the years passed and after my initial fear of being sent away from home, I grew to look forward to these trips to the farm. I liked the animals, enjoyed my time in the country, and began to think of myself as a farm boy.

I worked on the farm for "Aunt Bell" and "Uncle Dell." I knew nothing about them when I first arrived. Like Helen, I'm not sure where or when my parents met them. They were not relatives, and they didn't treat me as if they were my second parents or grandparents. They were simply my custodians for the summer, and I worked on the farm and did chores to earn my keep.

Just like the horses I had befriended in the streets of Chicago, I grew to love being around the farm animals every day. I was thrilled by the chance to work with them, and I believed they loved me in return. Even at that young age, I knew I wanted to spend my life working with animals.

On the farm, I learned to harness horses, feed all the livestock, and milk the cows. After each milking, we carried the pails of rich, creamy cow's milk from the barn to the milk house. There, we poured each pail into the cream separator. We cranked a wooden handle on the separator, it spun, and the centrifugal force separated the cream from the milk. We kept the milk for use in the kitchen and sold the cream to a local dairy. I also raked hay, gathered eggs, and served as the water boy for the threshers. It seemed something exciting happened each day on the farm.

The farm did not have any running water or indoor plumbing, so the family washed up for meals using a pan of warm water Aunt Bell had put out for that purpose. Each Wednesday and Saturday, everyone took a bath in a wooden tub in the milk house. The milk house had to be kept immaculate and was by far the cleanest outbuilding on the farm. It was also the closest to the house, which made it handy for us to take our baths.

Aunt Bell filled the big wooden tub about half full with warm water, and we lined up to take our turns. The first person in line stepped into the tub and got wet, stepped out of the tub, soaped up, got back into the tub, and rinsed off. Because we didn't have fluffy towels, we dripped dry.

If Aunt Bell and Uncle Dell had guests, they gave them the privilege of being the first in the bath. The last person to bathe that day didn't feel quite as clean afterward as the first person did. You can probably imagine how dirty a farmer can get from Saturday to Wednesday, and an eight-year-old boy can get even dirtier. After everyone was clean, we hung the wooden tub back on the wall of the milk house to dry, waiting for the next round of baths.

Aunt Bell and Uncle Dell didn't get many visitors, except maybe on Sundays, when most of the farmers took a rest from their work. On that day, families visited with one another after church.

It was exciting when the bread man came roaring down the lane on Wednesdays. Although he was called "the bread man," he sold much more than bread. Each of his visits lasted about fifteen minutes as he tried to sell Aunt Bell his wares. On his truck he carried small pots and pans, kitchen utensils, small packaged cakes, raw popcorn, and other treats. I enjoyed listening in on the adults' conversations, but I was especially excited if I had a little change in my pocket. Each week, Helen sent me a little note and usually enclosed a few coins. I spent these on Kool-Aid.

In Chicago, if someone offered us Kool-Aid with a meal, we felt as though we had died and gone to heaven. But on the farm, I could buy as much Kool-Aid as I could afford at three packages for a dime. The bread man sold other inexpensive treats as well, and I'll never forget the joy of having a little money to spend on myself. The bread man's visits made a big impression on me that I will never forget.

I remember one other visitor on the farm—one whom I did not look forward to seeing. For reasons I never knew, my parents sent my big sister, Lee Ann, down to the farm. Maybe it was a financial decision. Maybe they had some duties to do with their church. Or maybe they grew weary of her bossy nature! While she was at the farm, she tried to take over just as she did at home. One day as I worked in the barn, she sought me out to give me some unsolicited "sisterly advice." Actually, she only used the opportunity to mouth off and give me grief—as the older child in our family, she took her role as the stronger, dominant child to heart.

Lee Ann wielded a great deal of influence over our parents and often seemed to control them in matters concerning me. She talked and nagged and complained about my behavior. Unfortunately for her, at that moment I was not in the mood to hear her nagging. I was hand-milking a cow, and as she prattled on, I pointed the cow's teat right at her big mouth and tried to drown her with the milk. She went on complaining, but at least I had a smile on my face.

As I look back, I realize that was supposed to be a great time in my young life—a time of learning, growing, and participating in experiences. I was doing all the chores on the farm and truly enjoying myself in the company of cows, pigs, chickens, and especially horses. But again I had a feeling of not belonging—of being a "fifth wheel."

Aunt Bell and Uncle Dell were kind, but they were not my family. My family was far away, yet I didn't feel as if I belonged with them either. I longed for the kind of life I knew other kids had. I wanted to be part of a family and feel as if I belonged.

Out on the farm, I had a lot of time to think about life and my place in it. However, my life was in Chicago most of the year, and the day before school started each fall, I was put onto the northbound bus for my journey "home."

CHAPTER 2
WORK: A WAY TO BELONG

FROM THE AGE of eight to about fifteen, I searched for a place to belong—a way to belong—and found it through hard work. I knew the importance of work, because it not only provided me with cash in my pockets but also gave me a purpose. Yes, I was still attending school, but schoolwork was something I did after my job, or early in the morning before school.

No one in my family reminded me to do my homework, much less helped me with it or asked to see it. If I had a problem with school or schoolwork, I was left to work it out on my own. Parent-teacher conferences didn't exist in those days, and even if they had, I doubt my parents would have attended. It's likely that no one would have cared if I had dropped out. At that time, school administrators didn't require permission from parents or reams of paperwork to allow a kid like me to skip school and go to work instead.

I learned early that I liked having my own money. The few coins Helen sent me from time to time were nice, but I found I could earn a few more coins of my own by working. I would do almost anything for money, from delivering flowers to shoveling snow. I was only ten years old when I started delivering costumes at night in Chicago.

In 1938, movie theaters were popping up all over the country, and going to the movies was a big event. Patrons saw not just one film but usually two or three short films as well, and during the intermission, groups of actors or dancers entertained the audience. I delivered freshly cleaned and repaired costumes to these entertainers each night.

No boy that young should have ever been on the Chicago streets after seven-thirty in the evening. However, the costume company did send along a pit bull to accompany me on the long walk from the company to the theater, but whether the fierce dog was for my safety or the safety of their costumes, I didn't know. Most of my deliveries were to a hotel near the movie theater, and this particular hotel had an attached garage where guests could park their cars. This garage also served as a hangout for some of Chicago's gangs. I had just been a few months old at the time of the famous St. Valentine's Day Massacre of 1929, but the fallout from the gang warfare of the 1920s still lingered in the streets; Prohibition had ended in 1933, and many gang members were looking for new, profitable criminal activity to take the place of illegal alcohol sales. Although I was only ten years old, I was savvy enough to know the dangers of these Depression-era street gangs, and I learned to steer clear when I saw gang members on my path, looking to steal my costumes to make a quick buck.

In the 1930s and '40s, brutal corruption was commonplace in Chicago. Many people believed the Chicago crime families had infiltrated the police and were influencing the local politicians. Murders and shakedowns of businesses were everyday occurrences. I remember seeing dead bodies in the streets, probably the victims of gang warfare. I saw things a young boy shouldn't, but I believed this inhumanity was just a part of life, and I was just another kid on the streets trying to earn some money.

It's hard to imagine what my parents would have done if they had any idea of where I was most nights or what I was doing. While most parents wanted to protect their children from such brutality and mayhem, I don't think my parents would have cared if they had known I was earning cash in a virtual war zone. In fact, they probably would have ordered me to turn over the money I earned.

From the age of ten until I graduated from high school, I worked seven days a week and usually didn't return home until 7:00 PM or later. My mother cooked supper each evening for my father and my sister, but when I got home, there was never a meal set aside for me—not even leftovers or scrapings from what the rest of the family had eaten. I usually ate cold cereal for my dinner and sat alone at the table. To me, the loneliness of that empty table night after night seemed almost as brutal as the rough streets of Chicago, yet I understood the cruelty of the streets. I never understood my brutal exclusion from the love of my family.

The few friendships I formed during this time were also brutal. A kid my age should have a group to run around with, a team to play ball with, and a best friend to get in trouble with. But I couldn't afford to cultivate deep friendships. A boy could pretend to be my friend one day, and the next day steal my job. In those days, earning money was more important to me than having friends, and I can't recall the name of any of the boys in my school I would have called my "friends."

As I grew older, I moved on from making deliveries to more labor-intensive work. In Chicago in those days, a boy could hold an adult job regardless of his age, if he was willing and able to do the work. I was used to hard work and long hours, as I had done jobs on the farm that most people would consider "adult" jobs. I could rake, lift and toss hay, shovel and haul manure, and carry heavy buckets of milk across the barnyard into the milk house. I wasn't afraid of large, imposing animals like the gentle milk cows or the hard-working horses on Uncle Dell and Aunt Bell's farm. In fact, I loved working with the animals, and I knew I was good at it. When it came to animals, I liked working with horses the best. To me, horses were the finest creatures on the earth, and I was drawn to their strong, noble forms and their fiery yet tender spirits.

During the 1930s in Chicago, only the affluent had cars and other vehicles. Most residents still used horses for transportation, and the streets were filled with carriages pulled by Morgans. Gentle Belgians were used to deliver milk and pull the wagons of salesmen. In the more industrialized areas, four- or six-horse hitches of Percherons or Clydesdales pulled heavy wagons. It was a great time for a horse-loving boy like me to be alive.

In addition to my talent for working with horses, I also discovered I had a talent for marketing myself. One day, I walked right into a riding stable and said, "I'm here for a job." When the stable manager asked if I knew how to ride, I quickly and firmly answered, "Yes, sir, I do."

In truth, I had ridden horses on the farm, but I really didn't know the intricacies of horseman-ship—as in diagonal for the trot or right lead for the canter. But my pockets were empty, I needed a job, and to answer "no" was just not an option that day. The stable manager told me a class was about to start. "Get a horse and go out with them," he said. Perhaps it was luck, or perhaps it was from years of watching horses and riders, but as God is my witness, I was able to saddle the horse, mount easily (with what must have seemed like years of practice), and perform all the maneuvers the instructor asked of me. I got the job.

Working at the stables not only allowed me to be near horses every day, but again opened my eyes to dubious and questionable "business" practices. During my employ at the stables, wild mustangs from the West would be brought to the Chicago stockyards. Horse brokers brought these high-spirited horses to the city to sell to gullible Midwesterners, but those who needed a horse for work or transportation were not impressed when they saw these wild horses thrashing around in the railroad cars, and wouldn't even think of purchasing an animal that was not yet broken. So the mustang brokers hired me and another kid to ride the horses through a chute, three foot wide by forty foot long.

We put a rope halter on the horses, mounted them bareback, rode them through the chute, and jumped off. After we did this, the brokers could then legally sell these wild mustangs as "ridden" horses. It was dishonest, and I felt sorry for the buyers whom the brokers scammed in the deal. However, I earned fifty cents a ride, I got to ride a horse, and I received a little pocket change. What could be better?

I kept my pockets jingling by working at the stables every day after school and on Saturdays and Sundays. Because I was the youngest instructor at the stables, I was given the debatable privilege of teaching the older folks who came in for lessons, while the older instructors assigned themselves to the young, pretty gals. One day, a middle-aged woman came in for a lesson, and the older boys thought it would be great fun to assign me to teach her. She told me her doctor had advised her to start riding to help with back pain. I found this curious, as I thought the bounce this woman would get in the saddle would be hard on her back. But my job was to ride with her, not to argue, so I took the task.

I helped the woman mount her horse, and we walked several blocks on the bridle path. As we moved along, she seemed to get a little faint and swooned in the saddle. I was afraid she was going to fall off of the horse, but she reached out and held onto my arm as she "recovered" from her faint. This woman came back week after week for her riding lessons, and after several trips down the bridle path I finally realized what was going on. This woman was getting aroused on the horse! Shame, shame.

I wasn't completely ignorant about sex, as my father had previously fulfilled his parental obligation and given me the "talk" about girls. I can remember his concise speech word for word: "If you mess with girls, two things will happen. The girl will get pregnant, or you will get a bad disease." That was it. Even though his words were not elaborate, they stayed with me and later served me well in life. Unfortunately, like most of the lessons my parents gave me, or didn't give me, I had to find out the details on my own.

I worked at the stables all through my high school years. The job opened doors for me, and I met people who offered to help and guide me. At that time in my life, things seemed pretty good. The smell of horse manure was my cure-all. As long as I could work with horses, the concerns about my family situation seemed secondary. Nothing had changed at home, but with the horses, I was home.

Like most young men, I spent most of my high school years trying to be "cool." I wanted to be involved in athletics, so I tried out for the football team. Unfortunately, going out for football required after-school practices, and I needed to keep working. I had to make a choice, and working always won out. Working provided the "wants" of life and not just the "needs." While my parents covered my basic needs of food, clothing, and shelter, I didn't receive an allowance, and there were things I simply *wanted*. When my sister wanted things, my parents provided them. When I wanted things, I had to find a way to provide them for myself. I wanted a tie, a white shirt, and a solid-colored flannel shirt to wear over it. That was cool. I wanted to go to the movies and buy Karamel Korn. That was cool. Working hard and keeping money in my pockets allowed me to be cool.

Students at the high school I attended were predominantly Jewish, and there I learned firsthand about the atrocities of the Holocaust. I saw many people in the city with German-inked tattoos and heard their stories of hunger, rape, gas chambers, and families being ripped apart. The older Jews who escaped cried for their missing loved ones. The younger members of the community were serious and devout in their beliefs.

The more I spoke with my Jewish neighbors, the more I wondered what I would do if I were ever put in their position. I imagined making a brave escape from my captors and being welcomed home by a loving family. Of course, I was young and had not yet grasped the hardship that precedes any escape plan. I had not considered the awful choices and consequences that accompany such bravery. I had no idea of the horrors of imprisonment or the natural human instinct for survival.

At the time, I knew that when I turned seventeen, I was going to make my escape. I was going to leave my family and go to a place where I belonged. I had no idea where that would be or when I might begin that journey, but I was determined to make it happen.

CHAPTER 3

· ·

FROM HIGH SCHOOL TO
THE BIG WORLD

I N THE SUMMER of 1944, while I was working at the riding stable, I met a man who had connections with the movie industry. Now, this was exciting! The very thought of the movies made my engine run. In the days before television, movies were the primary entertainment for Americans, and everyone had their favorite stars.

I was hired to take a load of eleven horses to Mackinac Island, Michigan, for the production of *This Time for Keeps*. The movie starred Esther Williams, Jimmy Durante, Lauritz Melchior, and little starlet Sharon McManus. As I look back, it is hard for me to believe that movie industry officials asked a sixteen-year-old boy to take a load of horses from Chicago to northern Michigan by himself. Either they had a lot of confidence in my skills, or they were running short on money and needed to take the cheapest route they could. After all, the movie company had built a brand-new swimming pool at the Grand Hotel just for Esther Williams' famous swimming scenes.

The gentleman who hired me had rented a special slatted-bed truck with a loading ramp to transport the horses. The drive was over 400 miles, around the southern tip of Lake Michigan, through the lower peninsula of Michigan north toward the island. I had to stop about halfway in the trip to feed and water the horses and let them out of the trailer for a bit of exercise. Finally, after twelve hours, we arrived at the ferry dock. I parked the truck, took six of the horses by their leads, loaded them onto the ferry, and tied their leads onto the boat rail, leaving the truck and remaining horses on shore until my return trip. The horses were jittery on the unfamiliar metal deck of the boat and I was jittery as well, as this was my first time on an expanse of water as massive and foreboding-looking as Lake Huron. After what seemed like an eternity on the ferry, somehow the horses and I made it across the lake.

I asked directions, then walked those six horses two by two to the permanent stable on the island and got them settled down. Then I went back across the lake for the other five horses that I had left in the truck. I got those five onto the ferry, prayed we would make it across again, and finally got them settled into the stable once we had made a successful crossing. After that, my time on Mackinac Island was a piece of cake. I cared for those eleven horses all by myself during the two and a half months the movie was being filmed. I fed them, groomed them, and cleaned up after them all by myself. For a sixteen-year-old boy who loved horses and movies, this was a dream job and a great summer vacation, but the sad truth was that I was all by myself.

I stayed alone in a small room with a bath that was located in the stable. My main job was to get the horses ready for the scenes in which they were needed and be there when they were finished to take them back to the stable. Every day, a production assistant would tell me how many horses to have ready, where to take them, and when to be there. A professional trainer would prepare and place the animals in the scenes, so most days I was free to explore the small but interesting island, which is a haven for horse lovers, as no cars are allowed on Mackinac, even to this day.

When I was not caring for the horses, I enjoyed talking to people who were visiting the island on vacation. Couples, happy families, and even the staff of the Grand Hotel were all excited, following the film crew around the island and hoping to get a glimpse of a movie star. I didn't have to jockey the adoring crowds, however, as the stars came looking for me! One evening, Jimmy Durante wanted to take a buggy ride around the beautiful island to take in the views, and his assistant asked me to drive him. I was a bit starstruck and tongue-tied when we set out, but he was a personable man, just as he appeared on screen, and was a pleasure to talk with. That buggy ride with a big star on a beautiful evening is something I will never forget.

I never did meet Esther Williams, who kept mostly to herself when not in front of the cameras. It was later revealed in the press that she had been pregnant during the filming of the movie, but sadly lost the baby. I did, however, meet the little starlet. Sharon McManus's mother asked me to accompany the little girl on a ride up to see the Indian village, a historical site and fishing camp where the Ojibwa had settled. When I asked if Sharon knew how to ride, Mrs. McManus quickly replied, "Oh, yes." It soon became evident that Sharon didn't know how to ride and was, in fact, uncomfortable on the horse, so we settled for walking the horses to the village and back. She was a nice girl, but I wondered how many times Mrs. McManus had encouraged her daughter to attempt something she really didn't want to do. Her hasty confirmation of Sharon's riding prowess reminded me of my own several years earlier, and I realized that this "stage mother" was good at marketing her daughter, just as I was at marketing myself.

Movie poster from *This Time for Keeps.*

After my summer in Michigan, I successfully returned to Chicago with the eleven horses in tow. Although I can't recall how much I was paid for my Mackinac adventure, I knew I had gained much more than cash. I had gained confidence in my abilities as a horseman and a swagger in my step as a kid who had rubbed elbows with movie stars. I started my junior year of high school, and each day after school, I would report to the stables, do my assigned chores, and long for a few moments to ride. One day while I worked at the stables, I was offered the opportunity to ride the best horse I had ever seen, a beautiful and spirited animal. I knew riding this horse would be a challenge of my skills, and I welcomed the chance. The stable manager said I could ride the horse the following Saturday morning, and I couldn't wait.

The Friday night before the big day, with the temperature bitterly low, I went on a hayride. When I went to bed that night, I shivered beneath my covers. I woke on Saturday morning feeling as if I was getting the flu, but I was excited about the upcoming ride. I remember going into the bathroom to get ready and standing up in the bathtub. The next thing I knew, my sister was dragging me into her room, where she put me into her bed. Apparently she heard me fall, and my body blocked the door. I assume it must have been difficult for her to get the door open and get me out of the bathroom, much less drag me into her room. Although I was in a sickness-induced haze, I remember feeling thankful for my sister. Unfortunately, this was the one and only kind thing I can remember Lee Ann ever doing for me.

I was unconscious with a high fever for the next day and a half. When I finally regained my senses, my parents moved me back into my small room at the rear of our apartment. The tiny room had originally been intended to house hired help, but since my parents didn't employ a maid or cleaning lady, they felt it was big enough for me.

They left me back there alone and rarely visited me. My father was working, and my mother was too involved in my sister's activities to spend much time with me.

My parents were also busy moving Lee Ann into a larger room, as she needed more space for all her things. I asked myself countless times *where* she got all of these "things." As far as I knew, Lee Ann didn't do any work outside of our apartment, and my parents provided everything she wanted. Again, I felt as if I were a burden to my family—a mistake who just filled space. Why wouldn't anyone pay attention to me even when I was ill?

I was ravaged by fever and pain, so much so that I could barely force myself to sit up in bed. I couldn't eat, and I lost twenty-five pounds before this mystery illness finally ended. During my confinement, my parents never called a doctor. They held to their belief that through "prayer, knowing, and understanding," all things would be made possible through God. While I would have loved to believe that my parents were down on their knees in the living room fervently praying for my recovery, my heart tells me this probably wasn't the case.

Although a physician never formally diagnosed my illness, a nurse in my parents' congregation (who was a convert to Christian Science) said after hearing of all my symptoms that she was fairly certain I had polio. In 1945, young people in this country were suffering from the worst polio epidemic since 1916. Only by some miracle did I make it through that horrible disease.

When I finally felt well enough to go back to school, I was gaunt and my clothes hung on me. I was far from "cool looking." I had some trouble getting around, so a teacher at school suggested I try braces on my legs. She thought my leg muscles must have atrophied and weakened, which was one of the common aftereffects of polio. This, of course, was a foolish suggestion, for no one in my family would ever pay for that kind of medical equipment, even if it led to my increased mobility and recuperation. But again, through some sort of miracle, I grew stronger day by day as my muscles strengthened and my pain decreased.

As I recovered from my illness, I became more determined to leave my family and find my place in the world. I was spurred on toward this goal by an experience at the Chicago Railroad Fair, held in the summer of 1948. To this day, this extravaganza is one of my greatest memories. The event was held in Burnham Park to celebrate the 100th anniversary of the railroads "opening the West." The fair included exhibits of historic trains, new trains, displays by railroad manufacturers, and an elaborate daily show called "Wheels A-Rolling."

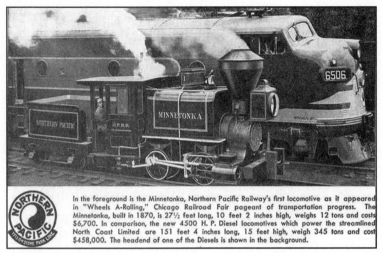

In the foreground is the Minnetonka, Northern Pacific Railway's first locomotive as it appeared in "Wheels A-Rolling," Chicago Railroad Fair pageant of transportation progress. The Minnetonka, built in 1870, is 27½ feet long, 10 feet 2 inches high, weighs 12 tons and costs $6,700. In comparison, the new 4500 H. P. Diesel locomotives which power the streamlined North Coast Limited are 151 feet 4 inches long, 15 feet high, weigh 345 tons and cost $458,000. The headend of one of the Diesels is shown in the background.

Postcard from Northern Pacific Railway.

The show was full of music, excitement, and fun. It portrayed the history of trains, beginning with the invention of the wheel, and their progression. The show began with an ox cart, featured a recreation of the Golden Spike ceremony that joined the East to the Far West, and ended with a fast train.

I learned the producers of the show needed trained horsemen to participate in the pageant. I was first in line. During different scenes I drove a covered wagon, a stagecoach, and a three-horse running fire engine. Because of my love and understanding of horses, I was given a huge amount of responsibility even though I was a young man. I relished every moment.

Graduate.

When I graduated from high school, I was ready to say good-bye to my family and go out on my own. Except for the roof over my head that my parents provided, I had practically been on my own since childhood. Now it was official.

Thanks to my Aunt Mary, my patron saint and guardian angel, I was able to enroll at a local junior college. Aunt Mary had made a good living running a mail-order business that sold false teeth. She guided and supported me throughout my teen years. In fact, she bought all my clothes. She owned three cars, even though I thought she was the worst driver in the state of Illinois. I learned from her the meaning of the phrase "white-knuckle driving." She lived the good life, and I am thankful she shared her good fortune with me.

After I graduated from Wilson Junior College in Chicago, Aunt Mary paid for my tuition to the University of Illinois. I was still crazy about horses, and I planned to study animal sciences and become a trainer. Unfortunately, the university horse barns burned down while I was there, and the school did not plan to rebuild them. I had no Plan B or firm goal, and I knew I didn't want to spend Aunt Mary's money on classes in which I had no interest, so I dropped out as a second-semester sophomore. Fortunately, my credits from junior college brought me up to a second-semester junior.

Always anxious to be around horses, I would go to any nearby stable, offering my services as a groom or stable boy. I attended horse shows around the Midwest and rubbed elbows with some of the most famous horsemen of the day. And those famous horsemen trained some of the most famous American Saddlebred horses of the time. It was through these associations that I met Bob Whitney, a man who had a great reputation for training young horses. He offered me a job at his stables in Muncie, Indiana, and I jumped at the chance to work with this master. Now officially on my own, I did as many young men did in those days—I rented a small room with a shared bath. I guess you could say I had made my first escape, but I was so alone.

I rode the bus every day to work at Whitney Stables. At the end of the route, I got off the bus and walked a mile to the stables, cutting through the pasture where I had met the blind mare. I always made it to work on time—"punctual" could have been my middle name. From the outside, it probably appeared as if I had an ideal life. I was a young man on his own working in the industry he loved. I worked hard and enjoyed it, but I stayed in the shadow of the horse industry. I was known as tough, timely, and dependable. This was becoming a pattern in my life.

College days.

I thought I had it made until late summer of my twenty-first year, when I received a letter from Uncle Sam. The letter said, "I need you." Three days before my twenty-second birthday, I left my small rented room to serve my country. I had survived the odyssey of childhood and my teen years, but now I had to face the great unknown. My new journey was about to begin.

CHAPTER 4

. . . .

A YOUNG SOLDIER LEARNS DISCIPLINE

WHAT DID THIS twenty-two-year-old new soldier know? I knew horses. I knew animals. I knew how to keep a little money in my pockets. Most of all, I knew how to make it on my own, stand on my own two feet, and be responsible for myself. That was the biggest lesson I had learned in my young life. Self-reliance was my best attribute.

But I quickly became good at something else: discipline. I believe self-reliance and discipline go hand in hand. To survive on the tough streets of Chicago, I not only had to rely upon myself, but I also had to learn to discipline myself. I had to put aside the things I wanted to do (spend money on "fun" things, play sports, date girls) and focus on the things I needed to do (work, save money, survive).

I also had to discipline my fears, as I wouldn't have been able to make it on the streets if I had given in to fears for my safety or even my life. Likewise, I had already conquered my fear of loneliness and had achieved the disciplines of instinct and wit. While wit was not a highly treasured attribute in a young recruit, the rest of these acquired skills soon proved to be a great benefit to me.

Until I joined the army, I never realized how much I craved the outside forces of discipline. When parents love their children, care about their moral upbringing, and work to give them tools for a successful life, they discipline them. Children may scream at their parents and shout, "You don't care!"—but that sort of discipline is a mark of caring mothers and fathers. It didn't take long for me to realize the army's discipline and structure had been missing in my life, and I thrived on those concepts.

I was sent to Fort Leonard Wood, located deep in the Ozark Mountains in Missouri. This base, which was the home of the Sixth Infantry, had almost become a ghost town after World War II. However, when operations escalated in Korea, they escalated at Fort Wood as well. I was at Fort Wood for sixteen weeks of Basic Training, and my life became all about "yes, sir" and "no, sir." In addition to discipline, we were taught how to shoot, throw hand grenades, fire artillery, and engage in a hundred other military techniques.

After Basic, I was chosen to continue my training at the Army Ranger School. I believe I was selected for this honor because of my athleticism. Although I had never been able to participate in high school sports, my various jobs involved physical activity, and despite my battle with polio, I was quick, strong, and fit. I also believe my self-reliance and discipline signaled something else to my superiors: leadership.

Army Rangers are known as take-charge men and have a long and proud history dating back to the Revolutionary War. Rangers earned their "special operations" honor in World War II when they scaled the high stone cliffs during the Normandy invasion. Their "brothers in arms" were the British Commandos, and the Rangers and Commandos became well-known for their daring accomplishments. Rangers were not needed much after the end of World War II, but when a war in Korea became imminent, army officials reinstated the Ranger School to prepare soldiers for the "extremely hazardous duty in the combat zone of the Far East."

I was sent to Fort Benning, Georgia, to complete the first step of my Ranger training. The instruction I received there was more in-depth and more intense than anything I had survived in Basic. I was trained in airborne jumps (including low-level night jumps), operations, demolitions, sabotage, close combat, and the use of foreign maps. I mastered all American small arms and received extensive training in communications.

My next stop was Fort Polk, Louisiana, where I completed more specialized training. Here I received the honor to be called an Army Ranger. I was now considered "Special Forces," and like the Green Berets, Navy Seals, and Delta Force, I was ready to go into a situation, swiftly take control by whatever means necessary, and get out as quickly as I had arrived. I was trained to subdue an enemy with little or no noise—a skill I didn't realize at the time would become a lifesaver for me. Of all the military training I received, the lessons I held closest in my mind and heart were to follow orders to the letter and always obey the last command first.

After my graduation from Ranger school, I was considered an MO (military operative). As I would soon learn, MOs were asked to do the impossible, and I would never have been able to get the job done without the strict Ranger training I had received. Now that I was part of the daring Ranger history, I was ready to go and get the job done. I knew I was prepared for whatever came my way. I was not, however, ready for my family's reaction to my new military career.

When I completed Ranger school, I was given a ten-day pass to visit my family, after which I was to report to Union Station in Chicago for departure to the "Far East Command." Everyone in America at that time knew this meant Korea. Everyone also knew that many of the young men sent there would not return home. Everyone in America was rallying around the troops—everyone, that is, except my family.

I returned to Chicago with no joy or fanfare. When I tried to tell my family of my accomplishments during combat training—I was quite proud (and perhaps a bit conceited) of my Ranger status—my family swiftly and silently ignored me. They had no interest in hearing my accounts of the training I had received or where I was headed next. Those ten days were not filled with pleasant visions of family meals around the table, conversation in the parlor, or the heartfelt tears and compassion one might associate with a family preparing to say good-bye to a son and brother—a son and brother they very well might never see again.

Instead, on the last day, I left the house alone. When I reached the train station, I saw it was filled with soldiers. Their girlfriends and families were bustling about, giving them hugs, kisses, and final good-byes. I found an out-of-the-way spot, dropped my duffle bag, and waited for the train. The scenes of sadness and love I saw taking place in front of me were almost too much for me to bear. Why was I alone? Why had no one bothered to accompany me to the station? Why had no one—my mother, father, or sister—even said good-bye? Why didn't I matter to them?

When the train finally arrived, I boarded it quickly so no one noticed the absence of my family or the tears in my eyes. Yes, I was a big, strong, smart, well-trained Army Ranger, but I was also a twenty-two-year-old boy who was leaving the only family he had ever known. Self-reliance and discipline are wonderful characteristics for a young man to possess, but a soldier needs to know that someone, somewhere, cares about him and his future. He needs to know someone is anxiously waiting for his return. Sadly, in my case, what this soldier needed and what this soldier got were two completely different things.

I was sad and depressed as the train rolled west. I guess you could say I was feeling so low that I could have walked under a snake while wearing a top hat. But I was still learning; I learned that the army was now my real family. The army fed me, housed me, clothed me, and, in a militaristic fashion, cared about me.

The one similarity I could see between my family back in Chicago and my army family was they both were teaching me not to get too close to others. We knew certain brothers in arms would not make it back home. I told myself this: "You, soldier, must continue to fight, despite missing your fallen friends, and despite the fact that you could be the next to fall and not make it home."

My army photograph.

CHAPTER 5

· ·

ACROSS MY COUNTRY, ACROSS THE SEA

F OR A YOUNG man who loved horses, the train trip from Chicago to Washington State should have been filled with daydreams of cattle drives across the plains and prairie nights around the fire. I wish I could have allowed the click-clack of the train wheels to lull me into sweet cowboy dreams, but I was sad about my family situation and needed to prepare myself for the next step.

Now a Ranger, I knew my missions in Korea—whatever and wherever they might be—would be treacherous. I also knew mental sharpness would be my closest friend. So, on that train, I decided to put aside my damaged family bonds and give my full concentration to the task ahead of me. When we disembarked in Washington, I felt that I was mentally ready for the odyssey I would soon be taking across the ocean. Unfortunately, my next step was not a pleasant one.

At every phase of military departures, a soldier's records are checked, rechecked, and then checked again. While I stood at what I thought was another routine check, the officers in charge discovered my shot record was incomplete. As much as I begged, pleaded, and tried to explain there had been some terrible mistake, they ordered me to the hospital, where I was administered eleven inoculations at one time. Although these preventatives were supposed to keep a soldier healthy, they just about did me in. I felt sick, weak, and disoriented.

Despite the discomfort I experienced from the inoculations, the officers still woke me at 2:00 the next morning. "Saddle up," they commanded. No one cared about my sore arms. We were moving out, and they needed to get us loaded aboard the navy ship that would carry us to Japan.

All soldiers climbed aboard the hulking gray behemoth of a boat. When we were all aboard, the army band on the dock played a rousing rendition of "So Long, It's Been Good to Know Ya." It seemed an odd and ominous choice for a bon voyage song, and we wondered if the band director knew something we didn't. I was assigned a berth on D-deck. I found my quarters and started to get my footing on this floating fort.

As the ship sailed into Puget Sound that foggy night and headed west to the Far East, we hit a tanker. Although we were soldiers and had been trained to deal with crisis situations on land, none of us were yet ready for a crisis on the water, and had never considered the possibility that our ship would hit another craft in Puget Sound. The boat lurched, alarms sounded, and then we heard over the loudspeakers, "Prepare to abandon ship!"

We knew what to do when we heard this warning, and we also knew "abandon ship" meant "get the heck off." We sprang into action.

D-deck was below water level, and the soldiers housed there were required to wear life vests. So, with hundreds of other soldiers, I scrambled up the staircases and vaulted feetfirst over the side. The trip from the topside of the ship into the ocean was a real doozy—much like a trip on an elevator that made a quick start when you weren't ready for it. The night was pitch black, I couldn't see the water, and I didn't know when I would splash down. Finally, after what seemed like a slow-motion movie scene, I hit the water like a rock. The water was extremely cold, and my shoes and uniform acted like sponges and soaked up the frigid water. I looked around me and saw that there were probably forty to fifty other soldiers in the water with me. If it weren't for the life jackets, many of us would have drowned.

I knew the ship personnel had scheduled a practice drill early into our voyage, but no one in the navy expected we would need that training on our first night at sea. I was not sure how to proceed, but I somehow found my way to the enormous rope ladders attached to the side of the ship. I grabbed a rope and hung onto those ladders with the multitude of other wet soldiers and awaited further instructions. These came in the form of a bawling-out by a navy brass, who bellowed, "We said to *prepare* to abandon ship." So we climbed back up the rope ladders, the freezing water cascading from the soaked uniform of one soldier onto the face and helmet of the one beneath. Sailors lined the railings, staring at us as if we were the stupidest folks in the world. They derided us the entire time we climbed. We felt pretty foolish, but I remember thinking, "Let's put those sailors in a foxhole and see what happens."

Our ship limped back to port in Washington, where we were transferred to a troop ship. This gigantic craft could have been called an iron castle, a steel hotel, or a medieval prison with hallways leading to dungeons. Yet the thing floated and carried thousands of American troops to do battle with the enemy. I quickly learned a new naval vocabulary: "aft" meant back, and "bow" meant front.

The ship was by no means a luxury liner. There were no chairs on deck—not even a place to sit your backside. Our sleeping quarters were below deck and consisted of canvas bunks attached to the wall, stacked four or five high. In the "sanitary facilities," thirty men sat back to back to do their business while water ran constantly below them—no flushing required. Getting "cleaned up" meant taking a saltwater shower that might feel a little warmer than it did the day before. All in all, the sixteen days I spent at sea made me long for the good old American farm outhouse.

It didn't take long for me to realize it was a good thing I was in the army and not the navy. The rolling thirty-foot ocean waves of the northern route to Japan left me sick and I could hardly eat. When we finally disembarked, I was glad to put my feet onto Japanese soil, regardless of what came next.

Troop ship bound for Korea.

CHAPTER 6

· ·

JAPAN TO KOREA

WE LANDED ON the eastern shore of Yokohama, located in the middle of the largest of the Japanese islands. We didn't have time for sightseeing as we immediately boarded a bus for Camp Drake, a United States Air Force facility located in Saitama, just outside of Tokyo. There we were given a bitter quinine pill (without water) to protect us from malaria, which had made many American soldiers sick.

The war was raging in Korea, so the next morning we boarded a train to Sasabo. From there, we took an overnight ferry to Pusan Harbor, Korea. The train ride from Tokyo to Sasabo was difficult. Imagine being a young American man of average height and weight and stepping onto a Japanese Pullman train designed to transport people of much smaller stature. We simply did not fit. Everything was too small, we were cramped, and it wasn't a pleasant ride. The ferry trip took all night, and we only had a grass mat on which to sleep. I remember thinking that these sleeping arrangements could never replace a Holiday Inn!

When I arrived in the Far East, I knew very little about the war or how it had started. Later in life I studied its history and understood what had led up to the conflict in Korea. I learned the war started on June 25, 1950, when North Korea invaded South Korea. Although the United States knew North Korea was building up its forces near the border, the invasion caught us and South Korea by surprise. President Truman had withdrawn the US Army from Korea to Japan in 1948, so we had no forces present in that country when the invasion took place.

Four days later, the South Korean capital of Seoul fell to the North Korean army. The next day a coalition of US, British, and Australian Army, Navy, and Air Force units rushed to South Korea's aid in an attempt to slow the invasion. Meanwhile, the US and its allies worked in the United Nations to get a resolution to defend South Korea.

Part of the problem in 1950 was that the US Army was in a much different state than it had been when it defeated Japan in World War II. The development of weapons for a ground war had stagnated. Military strategists had concluded that because of the existence of atomic weapons, extended ground wars were now a thing of the past. The US had also been steadily decreasing its troop levels in the region since the time the Japanese surrendered five years earlier, so the units sent to aid South Korea were undermanned and, for the most part, had access to only antiquated weapons from World War II.

By August 4, more than 140,000 Republic of Korea (a.k.a. South Korea), American, British, and Australian troops had been pushed into the "Pusan Perimeter," which was a stretch of territory around the port city of Pusan on the southeast coast of South Korea. The troops fought off repeated attacks by the North Korean Army (NKA) until September 18.

On September 15, Allied forces led by General Douglas MacArthur landed at the port of Inchon. This bold invasion behind NKA lines surprised the North Koreans. As the Allied forces broke out of Inchon and the Pusan Perimeter, thousands of exhausted and decimated NKA regulars realized they were in danger of being trapped. Just as fast as the NKA forces had swept through South Korea in June, they now headed back north to escape destruction at the hands of the Allied forces.

On September 29, the Allies recaptured Seoul, forcing the NKA to continue its flight to the north. Less than two weeks later, on October 9, the Allies made the fateful decision to cross the 38th parallel and invade North Korea. This action alarmed the Chinese Communist Forces, and by October 14 they were moving into North Korea to support their neighbor and ally. On October 19, the allies captured Pyongyang, the capital of North Korea, and continued advancing until they reached the Yalu River (the border between North Korea and China) in late November 1950.

At this point the Allies were confronted with the "human wave" attacks of the Chinese, and by December 31 that nation was pouring an additional 500,000 fighting men into North Korea. By the time the American troops (both marine and army) pushed as far north as the Chosin Reservoir, the temperature was -50°F, the coldest in North Korea's history. It soon became apparent the American forces were ill-prepared for the brutal cold and the rough Korean terrain. Vehicles were not available, so many soldiers marched into battle, not knowing the price their bodies were about to pay.

The Chinese and North Koreans took advantage of the American forces' disarray and tried to push them into the sea. As the push continued, thousands of troops walked toward the port city of Hungnam to escape the enemy. While US troops fled, the USS *Missouri* provided cover for the retreating marine and army troops. The USS *Missouri* was an Iowa-class battleship, displacing 60,000 tons, and could travel at speeds up to thirty-five knots (fifty-eight miles per hour). Commissioned on June 11, 1944, it was most famous as the site of the surrender of the Japanese at the end of World War II, the document of which was signed on its deck on September 2, 1945, in Tokyo Bay.

To protect the troops, the navy laid down a ring of fire using the battleship's sixteen-inch guns, which was effective in keeping the Chinese from entering the city of Hungnam. The shells weighed 2,700 pounds each and had a range of twenty-three miles. Each shell could leave a hole in the ground as big as a house.

Now that the troops were fairly well protected, the weather became the main concern. The army had issued insulated shoe packs to the soldiers, but in many ways these proved to be as dangerous as the enemy. The packs were basically two pieces of felt, and when that felt became wet, frostbite was inevitable. Frostbite was especially insidious because as it took hold the soldiers' feet got numb, but they were otherwise unaware of what was happening. As a result, hundreds of the thousands of fleeing marine and army personnel were afflicted, and surgeons had to amputate thousands of toes and feet. It was a bitter way for men to become casualties of the war.

It took the navy a day and a half of constant troop movements to save the soldiers who retreated.

The navy was on battle stations for thirty-six hours, with the USS *Missouri* serving as the flagship of the battle group. By Christmas Eve, 105,000 American and Korean troops (along with their equipment) and 91,000 Korean civilians had been sealifted to Pusan. The rout was on. The Chinese and NKA pushed the underequipped and outnumbered Allies south. On January 3, 1951, the Allied forces abandoned Seoul, and the city once again fell to the NKA/Chinese forces.

On January 25, 1951, the Allied forces launched Operation Thunderbolt and went back on the offensive. By March 15, the Allies had recaptured Seoul. In April, President Truman relieved General MacArthur of command for publicly questioning and disagreeing with him. He was replaced by General Matthew Ridgway.

I arrived in Korea in May of 1951. History books say that by that time the forces were roughly stalemated and truce talks began in July 1951. However, "stalemate" does not mean vacation. The two sides ended up being locked in negotiations for almost two years. Fighting continued and became a massive defensive struggle, with little ground gained by either side. Each time one side attempted an offensive strategy, it was met with great loss of life. This was my Korean War, and one that continued in stubborn fashion until the Armistice was eventually signed on July 27, 1953.

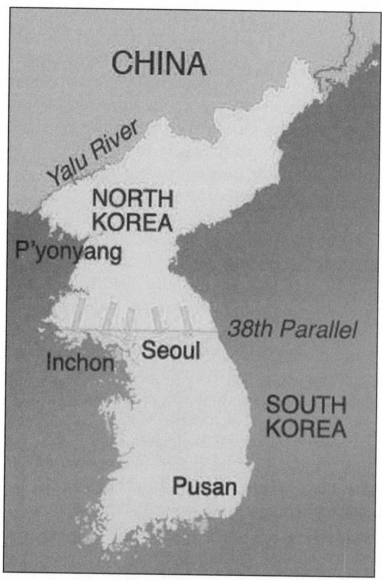

Map of Korea.

After my group arrived in Pusan Harbor in 1951, we were put into a barbed-wire enclosure to await orders for the trip north. The experience up to this point had been traumatic for us, as most of us were in a foreign country for the first time and didn't know quite what to make of it all. The past twenty days had been exhausting—a shipwreck, ocean travel on rough seas and the accompanying seasickness, crowded train rides, and, for me, eleven shots at one time. Now, from our barbed-wire enclosure, we watched as people carried "honey buckets" full of human waste away from homes. This was the sanitation system in Korea. We felt as if we had landed in a primitive time.

We were soon loaded onto boxcars according to our destination. The boxcars were small and travelled on narrow gauge track. Again, comfort was not a priority. I sat on the floor and leaned against the wall, and our only bathroom facility was a hole cut into the floor. As we proceeded north, we had to stop at each tunnel so the South Korean army could check for explosives.

At one tunnel, we waited for another train to pass that was headed south. Although it looked like just another boxcar, we immediately recognized it as a medical train filled with stretchers laden down with wounded South Koreans. The Korean hospital train stopped next to our car, and for the first time we were face to face with wounded soldiers. Bloody bandages, broken arms, missing legs—it was suddenly very real. Although I was well trained and perhaps better prepared for this sight than many of the Regular Army in our car, I still had to swallow hard and gather my composure when the reality of war was right in my face. We were headed north, from where these soldiers had just come.

I wondered about these soldiers: Who would help them? Who would care for their wounds? South Korea was a poor country. Would there be enough doctors? How many would survive? My thoughts took on a more personal tone: How many of us on this boxcar would be wounded? How many of us would be killed? Slowly, a creeping message made its way into my mind: What about tomorrow? Up to this point I had thought about the possibility of being killed, but I had never considered that I might be wounded.

My thoughts turned toward home and my lonely departure from Chicago, and I realized that even in that boxcar full of American soldiers, I was alone. Who would accept my body if I were killed? Who would hold my dog tags in their hands and say, "He was mine"? I had put my family into the far reaches of my brain on that train ride across the plains of America, but now I came to a stark realization: If the army was my family, where was my home? In this boxcar? In Chicago?

I had no connection and no history—only a future in Korea.

CHAPTER 7
TO THE NORTH

MY GROUP CONTINUED north for assignment to units. For security reasons, I never
knew my own MOS (military operative
status), though it had long before been decided.
The brass knew I was an Army Ranger, and there
would be particular locations just for me.

I was assigned to both the 2nd Infantry Division
(called "The Indian Head Division" because of
the black-and-white patch they wore) and the
7th Armored Division (who wore a red-and-black
patch). However, I was on "detached service,"
which meant I had no total unit involvement and
worked for both divisions (sometimes simultane-
ously). One day, I would be given a clean shirt with
the Indian Head patch; the next day (or the next
time we got clean laundry), I would receive a shirt

with the emblem of the 7th Division. My job was to go where I was needed. This also meant I had no real home, which, of course, reminded me of my civilian situation.

I was a forward observer, commonly referred to as an "FO." In general, an FO was, as the name implies, positioned out in front of the combat infantry and artillery. Many history books refer to the Korean War as the "Artillery War" because of the more than sixty different US artillery battalions that served on the Korean peninsula during the course of the conflict.

As the infantry was ordered forward, the officers depended on the FO to determine the presence of the enemy, either by sight or by hearing their movements, and call in positions so the officers knew where to lay down the artillery fire. One call from an FO could bring down tremendous firepower onto a specific site. In this way, the troops could proceed.

As an FO, I kept myself hidden and got into position at night. I pulled wire along with me in order to communicate with the officers who planned the maneuvers. I wrapped two wires around my waist and tied them securely, or carried a wire in each fist as I made my way to my hidden location. Once there, I attached the wires to an EE8-A military field phone, hooked it up, cranked the device for power, and then prayed somebody answered. If someone did, I relayed the information I knew; but if no one answered, I had big problems. Several times in my career as a forward observer, the phone wire broke somewhere between me and the officers who were awaiting my direction. It might have gotten snagged on a rock, stepped on by another soldier, or actually found by the enemy and destroyed, thus severing communications. There was absolutely nothing I could do in this situation, as it probably would have been a fatal decision to backtrack and locate the break. If the artillery batteries didn't hear from me, they knew that either the wires had been broken or I was dead. Depending upon the strategy and goal of that particular skirmish with the North Koreans, US artillery sometimes opened fire, leaving me in an extremely precarious position, usually scrambling for cover.

Cranking the noisy phone was another issue. With artillery exploding everywhere, it wasn't heard, but in the quiet of night I was always concerned that the noisy operation would give away my position.

EE8-A.

If a soldier had a choice of his activity in the army, I suggest he not be an FO. I was exposed to both sides—mine and theirs—and when either side made a decision to move, I was surrounded by chaos. The chaos raged inside me as well. Although I had been trained for these situations, it was still frightening. I am grateful my adrenalin saw me through many tough situations—situations I don't know how I could have survived otherwise.

Many FOs in the field were forced to make the fateful decision to call artillery down on themselves in an effort to hold back the enemy and allow the Allied troops to take the ground. These FOs were heroic young men who accepted and fulfilled a duty that was often a death sentence. Twice in my assignment as an FO I had to call in artillery on my own position, but somehow I survived.

When I first arrived at the 2nd Infantry Division, it was "on line" and receiving heavy casualties. The division often lost ten to thirty men in an assault. I never had time to unpack. I was briefed, and within thirty-six hours I was in heavy combat.

We were headed north to the 38th parallel—an invisible "line in the sand" that became well-known to Americans who read dispatches from the war. The 38th parallel separated the industrialized north of Korea from the agricultural south. I was kept busy serving two units heavily engaged in battle in this area. When I wasn't with one unit, I was pressed into service with the other. Being on detached service gave me little time to wonder what could happen next.

Foot soldiers like me were never privileged to see the big picture, so I didn't know exactly where we were geographically or the goal of the particular maneuver in which I was engaged. I worked from one day to the next, following orders and doing my best to stay alive. I remember crossing the 38th parallel one time and being driven back when the Chinese entered and joined the North Koreans. I saw the Chosin Reservoir once from a plane. I never knew exactly what significance any battle or operation had on the overall history of the conflict.

The big picture was huge. Little did we realize we were in the middle of what would one day be referred to as "historical combat" north of the 38th parallel. We never knew major battles such as Heartbreak Ridge, Old Baldy (which was once a tree-covered mountain but was left battle scarred with only stumps), and Hill 47 were happening all around us. Soldiers are supposed to follow orders, and for me that meant calling in artillery. Doing so in the mountainous area around the 38th parallel was like playing the violin without a bow. FOs were expected to produce good results without the tools needed to do so. For this reason, the artillery calls were often too short or too long.

South Korean civilians used A-frames to get the ammunition up the steep, mountainous inclines to the front where it was needed. The men placed hemp straps over their shoulders, pulled on these straps, leaned slightly forward until the legs of the frame came off the ground, and then away they went. The men who moved the supplies usually were small in stature, and as they walked single file over the rough terrain, the A-frame was just a little shorter than the man using it. These men carried four times their own weight. They were valuable tools in ensuring there was enough ammo at all times for the missions.

Korea was a rugged and primitive country. There were no paved roads, no electric lights, no

Korean soldier with an A-frame on his back.

wooden houses, no running water, and, of course, no sanitation. In some instances, the place was downright ugly. We watched in disbelief as the Koreans used human waste as fertilizer on their fields and gardens. Bugs, lice, and mosquitoes were commonplace, and the civilians ate whatever was available. After a monsoon the roads were washed out, and we sometimes saw an arm or leg sticking out from the mud. Because these were Korean soldiers and not Americans, a bulldozer came and pushed earth over the remains.

On occasion I would go out with an infantry squad of twelve men on reconnaissance missions. These missions were primarily to inspect the terrain and try to detect troop movements in the area. We patrolled in single file or in a loose V-formation. During one of these patrols, the squad leader (a lieutenant) threw his fist into the air, which we immediately translated as, "Danger—movement ahead." We all froze in place. The lieutenant's next gesture sent two men to his right and two to his left, while the rest of us remained as silent and unmoving as stone.

The two soldiers on the right saw a small boy sitting beside a motionless body. We carefully advanced and found the boy sitting next to a woman, who we assumed was his mother. She appeared to have been dead for several days, and the little boy—who was probably around five years old—was out of his mind with fear. I approached him with my hands extended in what I hoped he saw as a symbol of caring. He seemed confused, and it was apparent he had not eaten, nor had any water or other comforts, for quite some time.

I picked up on a faint glimmer of recognition in the boy that I did not intend him harm and continued my slow approach. I tried to remember what it was like to be a little five-year-old boy, but my heart was nearly pounding out of my chest—I knew it was a miracle for him to be alive in such a horrible environment. For a moment, I wondered if perhaps God had brought me on this path to find him.

GIs always carry along something to eat—crackers, cookies, or candy. I gathered what the other soldiers had on them and made an offering to the boy. He took a cookie, and I wondered if perhaps it seemed a familiar food to him. He choked on it and we assumed he probably hadn't eaten real food in quite some time, as he seemed to find it hard to swallow. We gave him water, and though no words were spoken, we definitely felt his "thank you" radiating from his dark, sincere eyes.

We buried his mother quickly and reverently, even though we knew nothing about her or her child. The little boy seemed drawn to me, so I took his hand in mine and started back to camp, which was about a mile away. At the time, I was in reserve (meaning I was on a "break" from my regular duties) and had some time to devote to him. He stuck close to me and slept next to my cot on the floor each night. That poor little boy, whom I christened "NoName," needed someone. I was that someone.

Unfortunately, our pleasant days together were short lived. Being in reserve is not like having vacation days, and soon I was called to another mission. Our few days together had brought me joy. Now, I felt as if my heart was being ripped from my chest to leave him. I felt guilty, as if I were abandoning him, even though I was following orders. The other soldiers promised they would care for the boy until a suitable place could be found for him to live. In some ways, I was glad we couldn't communicate verbally, as I fear NoName's words upon my departure might have killed me.

Me and NoName. I cherish this photo.

I never saw the boy again, but I

have thought about him at least a million times over the years and have wondered what his future held. I longed for one more glimpse of him, thinking that would ease my pain. In my heart, that little boy was mine. I had been the first to hold his hand after his mother died. I had been the first to comfort him and the first to give him real GI food. He was my "first child," and I felt as though I had failed him.

CHAPTER 8

· ·

A CASUALTY OF WAR

MOVING FROM ONE division to another gave me little time to rest, but I was never alone and never in need of something to do. I have many memories of the battles in which I fought. One such memory is of a time the North Koreans were mounting a major assault. From my position as FO, I could see thousands of enemy soldiers crossing an open area, so I immediately called for TOT (time on target). This meant every US artillery weapon in the area would fire, spaced so the shells landed in that open area at the same time.

To explain this further, imagine a division has four artillery batteries (units of guns, mortars, rockets, and missiles). Each of these divisions could consist of one 155mm battery and three 105mm batteries. If Command orders to fire a TOT, the artillerymen in each battery use the information provided by the FO to determine the location of their coverage. The men know how much powder it will take to get the shell to that location so that their shells will arrive at the same time as the shells from the other batteries in the division. In this instance the whole area filled with gray smoke, and when it lifted I saw hundreds of soldiers down on the ground, with many others walking around as if they were in a trance. It was like something out of a nightmare.

For personal use, the weapon of choice for most army personnel was the M1 carbine. This weapon was lightweight and carried a clip containing fifteen rounds of ammo. Compared to the carbine, the M1 rifle was heavy and held only seven rounds of ammo in its clip. Although a soldier could hit a target at 300 yards with the M1 rifle, most found the carbine to be better suited for combat or house-to-house situations. In one battle, I saw a soldier running with a carbine on his shoulder. A moment later he was hit by artillery. The man wasn't hit, but his weapon was gone. The concussion from the bomb caused him to lose his weapon, but not his life. I was beginning to believe in miracles.

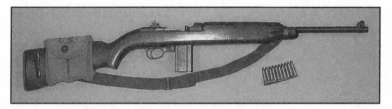

Korean War-era M1 carbine.

On one mission, I was involved in what was known as a "snatch and run." The army believed that some GIs were being held in one of three hooches in a location fairly close to our position. We took two half-tracks (half tank, half truck), each mounted with two 30-caliber machine guns, and made our way to the site. The lieutenant in charge halted the half-tracks about a thousand yards from the hooches and ordered the gunners to fire on anything that moved. The rest of us were to grab the prisoners and get out. I am proud to say that when the operation was over, we had rescued six GIs. I never got to speak with these men and knew nothing of their ordeal, but I was proud to have been a part of their rescue.

On another occasion, our forces were being hit hard and air support was called in. As the planes flew over our line, one of our pilots fired a few seconds too soon. Although our soldiers were lying as flat as they could on the ground, one soldier—a farm boy from Illinois like me—took a hit. The round tore a big hole in his upper leg and blew off his testicles. He was in bad shape and had to be airlifted to Japan via MASH in an airborne hospital plane.

I know where this boy was taken because a few days later I suffered wounds from a mortar attack and had to be airlifted to the same hospital. I met up with him, and it was not long after that his voice began to change—a horrible and ever-present result of his injury. That boy had visions of being a good citizen, a contributor to his community, and a husband and a father. He had visions of having a good life, but all of those beautiful dreams were blown away on that hilltop in Korea. I felt deeply for him and knew I could have suffered the same fate.

My injuries occurred in midsummer, sometime during July 1951, two or three months after I arrived. I was with some other soldiers in reserve, and we thought we were in a safe area when mortars dropped on our left side. I was hit in the left forearm, right leg, and torso, and on my eyebrow and scalp. The arm and head injuries were superficial, but the ones to my leg and torso were more serious. I was taken by helicopter to a MASH unit, where the surgeons operated on me under morphine—I was not completely anaesthetized.

In my drug-induced state, I heard a sound that brought back a memory, a time when my mother took me to a butcher shop and ordered a slice of ham. The butcher picked up a stainless steel saw and cut through the bone. When I looked at the operating table next to me, I noticed they were taking off a soldier's leg with the same type of saw. Luckily, that was all I remembered until I was in recovery.

After my surgery, I asked a corpsman, "What did they do to me?" He checked my chart and replied, "I think they short-gutted you." I didn't know what that meant at the time, but I later learned that because of where I had been hit, the doctors had been forced to remove some of my small intestines. When I think of the Illinois boy and the man on the surgery table next to me, I count myself lucky.

I had a relatively short stay in Japan, and I was allowed to leave the hospital when I was on my feet and feeling better. One day I went to the Daiichi Building, where Command had its headquarters. I passed an officer, but I did not salute. I can't tell you why—as a Ranger and a soldier, I always took orders and protocol to heart. The officer stopped me and asked why I had failed to salute. I didn't have an answer, so he wrote me up. Perhaps it was the trauma of battle or my injuries that had fogged my brain and caused my lapse and my lack of a good response.

One evening I went to a dance sponsored by Command, where I met a lovely Japanese girl named Fumiko. We slow-danced, and the next day we met in downtown Tokyo. She and I, along with other soldiers and Japanese girls, went to the zoo. Yes, I was a real swinger! The zoo was small, and the first thing I saw was a Holstein cow, which reminded me of home and the farm. Then I saw a ragged baboon with a red behind, and then a lion with mange. Although it was good to be back in civilization, I wish I had not gone to the zoo that day—it was a desperate and sad sight. In the middle of war, nothing is really "fun," especially trying to talk pidgin English to a pretty girl and attempting to explain the humor in a Holstein cow and a worn-out old ape. It took the joy right out of that day.

Command soon determined that my injuries were healing well and I should return to Korea. Many FOs had been killed in the line of duty, and I was desperately needed back at the front.

During my time in the army, I did not forget the lessons I had learned on the streets of Chicago. I was never one to pass up an opportunity—especially the opportunity to line my pockets. One day, as the time drew near for me to go back, I hired a cab

My translator and me. The South Korean army usually furnished FOs with a translator.

to take me to a black market area in Tokyo. I knew the troops in Korea would almost kill for alcohol, so I wanted to buy a case of whiskey and sell it to them. Despite many problems, I got the whiskey back to Korea and made some money on the deal.

I had learned early in my military service that I could use my ration certificates to my advantage. As I went up in rank, I started getting a beer ration and the K-ration cigarettes. I sold my rations and sent the money to my account in the United States. By the time I got back home, I had saved enough money from selling beer and cigarettes to be able to pay cash for a Pontiac.

After I returned to Korea, I began having problems with my wisdom teeth. I took some pain medicine, but it didn't help. So I went to a MASH unit and asked to see a dentist. The dentist looked in my mouth and asked, "How bad are you hurting?"

I replied, "Pretty darn bad."

The dentist told me that a recent monsoon had delayed the shipment of supplies, and there was no Novocain for my tooth extraction. I had two choices: he could pull the teeth without Novocain, or I could keep hurting.

I knew I might not be able to return to a MASH unit for some time after I reported back to my unit, so I said, "Let's do it." I prepared myself for the worst.

The dentist's section of the MASH tent had not yet been prepared, so we took the steel dental chair outside to a flat area. "Hang on, soldier," he said. "Here we go." He was a short man and had to get a box to stand on, but he extracted my wisdom teeth in fairly quick fashion. He gave me some pain pills, but I know that when I left the MASH unit I probably resembled a whipped puppy.

I returned to my unit in early October. The weather had started to change, and on some mornings there was frost on the ground. Turkeys had been delivered for our Thanksgiving dinner, and the troops immediately buried them deep in the ground to slow the thawing process. But the Koreans discovered they were there, and our Thanksgiving turkeys disappeared. We never knew if it was the North or the South Koreans who took them, but we had no birds for our GI Thanksgiving dinner. I guess the Koreans weren't ones to pass up an opportunity either.

CHAPTER 9

CAPTURE

I N THE NORTH, things were heating up. From my position as an FO, I covertly watched as the North Korean Army began a buildup of equipment, and I knew something big was on the horizon. I was serving with the 7th Division when we received orders to move. Our position was again to be in the rugged, mountainous regions, fighting on solid rock. The 1st Marine Division was to be on our right flank. We had two battalions on line, and the marines had two battalions up front. As an FO, part of my job was to determine the strength of the North Korean artillery, as we knew they would use the large number of artillery pieces they had assembled to soften our side. We discovered that while they had assembled more men, they had not amassed the heavy weapons one would expect to launch a massive attack.

The buildup of forces continued for two weeks, and frost began to cover the ground each morning as the dreaded Korean winter crept up on us. The anticipation of battle was thick in the air and visible in the eyes of my fellow soldiers. We didn't know where we were in North Korea and we didn't know the battle plan, but we did know that we would soon be ordered into combat.

Any time an army on the offensive begins an assault, they have to make sure the first contact is as brutal as possible. The goal is to "soften the enemy," meaning the army kills as many of the enemy as possible. The second goal is to remove the enemy from high ground, as in military history the army that controls the high ground is usually the one that wins the battle. In Korea, this was especially important because of the rocky, mountainous terrain. If we could hold the hill (or mountain), the soldiers attempting to take our position would tire more quickly as they fought uphill. They also had little visibility, and it was difficult for one soldier to see anything but the next soldier in front of him. On top of the hill, the visibility is far better.

As I explained earlier, communications between the FOs and Command were iffy at best. During this battle, communications were nonexistent because we had no command center. No wires had been pulled, which meant no phones could be used. We relied solely on visual contact and were at the mercy of our hilly surroundings. The North Koreans had no hard-wired communications either, but they used bugle calls that told the troops the direction in which to proceed.

The North Koreans repeatedly struck the US Marines with wave upon wave of soldiers and eventually overran the line the marines were defending. Our position divided into splinter groups, and the North Koreans started dismantling our big weapons to make them unusable. The scene quickly descended into mayhem. It was literally impossible to know who was in charge or what our orders could be.

I hunkered down, but the Allied troops were like ducks on a pond—easy to spot and easy to shoot. We were trapped in a low spot between hills. Just like in the cowboy movies I had enjoyed as a kid, we were surrounded with no place to run and no hope of escape. By the time the shelling ended, I knew most of our troops had retreated. I hid for one horrible night in the craggy mountains, but at the break of day the North Koreans patrolled the area and ferreted out any prisoners they could find. I was captured along with thirty-six other men from various UN forces. I believe if we would have been on flat land, our chances of avoiding capture would have been much better, for on flat land we would have been able to see, run, and return fire. Here in the mountains the North Koreans knew so well, we were easy prey.

The North Koreans, however, seemed unprepared to take in prisoners. After a painfully long and confusing time of listening to our captors argue about us (and not understanding a word they were saying), we were marched for approximately two and a half hours and finally arrived at some sort of compound. This was not a typical North Korean/Chinese prison camp that we had all been briefed about in our training. This prison was a thatch-roofed mud hut, which we soon and "affectionately" referred to as the Hooch.

The "prison guards" were young and immature North Korean boys whose thin bodies were swimming in their soldiers' uniforms. The regular soldiers returned to the battlefield, leaving these young guards in charge. I quickly came to understand that, their military costumes aside, they, like me, were nothing but farm boys. But they had the guns, and there was no way to escape. We waited to see what would happen, as the guards seemed unsure of how to proceed with their new prisoners.

Later that evening, our situation took another serious turn when the North Korean soldiers came back to the camp bearing lanterns. They made us take off everything above the waist, and then they tattooed each of us with a number on our left shoulders. The North Koreans had a book with English numbers, a needle, and an inkwell. I was tattooed with the number 31. These numbers were the only attempt our captors made at using English. The soldiers and guards spoke no English, and no one in our group spoke Korean. When the regular North Korean soldiers left the compound, the guards—who seemed to be left to their own devices—communicated to us through gestures, pushing, grunts, yelling, and punches, and this primitive language soon became our only exchange.

During the first few days of our capture, I studied the guards to determine who were the more hostile and who were less likely to kill us. It didn't take long for me to realize these young boys were out of their league. I guessed their training was minimal. In fact, the North Korean soldiers probably gave them a weapon and told them to guard us. It seemed they made up the rules for guarding prisoners of war as they went along.

For the first few days, we were forced to remove our shirts and coats and line up by the numbers tattooed on our arms. However, this roll call proved to be too difficult for the guards, as they could not understand enough from the English book to line us up in numerical order. Their frustration showed. After the first few attempts, they simply counted the thirty-seven of us and were satisfied. This satisfied us, as well, for we were no longer forced to remove our warm clothing and stand shivering in the frigid air as they spent hours attempting to translate the book they had been left. With no understanding of Arabic numbers, it was impossible for them to line us up as they had been ordered to do.

The Korean winter was bitterly cold, and we suffered every day and night of our capture. The food the guards gave us once each day was a watery mixture we couldn't name, but it smelled and tasted vaguely of garlic, cabbage, or fish.

If the guards thought playing soldier was an adventure, the shine of it wore off quickly. They soon became as disenchanted with the cold and miserable situation as we were. Their individual mean streaks began to show, and they herded us around like cattle and treated us like the pigs on their farms. We knew if the shoe were on the other foot and we were the ones in charge, we would have fed and housed them in a humane manner. The North Koreans had no such compassion.

I continued to watch our captors, giving them little "tests" in my mind. I paid close attention to which boy was considered to be the leader and which were simply following orders. Because I couldn't understand their language, I paid careful attention to body language and looked for clues about the nature of their mission. I watched which boy stood straighter and which boys slumped in his presence. I watched which boys waved their hands and arms about as they talked, and which kept their hands to their sides. I could soon pick out the leaders of the guards, but I needed more information that seemed to be impossible to attain just by watching. I wanted to know what they were going to do with us, and when they were planning to do it. Although I was only twenty-two, my training as a Ranger was kicking in. I tried to act less like a boy and more like a man of thirty.

As the days passed, it became clear the North Koreans had no idea of what to do with their group of prisoners. So in the Hooch we structured a sort of daily routine to allow us to stay physically fit and alert. Although it would have been easier for us to cocoon ourselves against the bitterly cold temperatures, we exercised in the Hooch. We couldn't move around too much—thirty-seven men doing calisthenics stirred up too much dust from the earthen floors—so we pranced about. Stepping high like a saddlebred horse without shuffling created less dust.

Because of the length of our capture, to this day I can recall every detail about the Hooch. We were being held in an oblong structure measuring approximately eighteen by thirty-six feet with dirt floors, mud and grass walls, no windows, and a hemp roof eight feet off the ground. The wooden rafters were approximately thirty inches on center and held up by tree trunks about twelve by sixteen inches in diameter. One of these trunks had been placed about every four feet. There were only two entrances: one at the rear of the structure, and one on the side about midway back. The guard's shacks were located just outside these entrances. If the Hooch had been a typical North Korean civilian family unit, it probably would have housed about four families. In the US, however, we would equate it to the size of a small school classroom. With thirty-seven men in the building, it felt less like a classroom and more like a crowded nightclub dance floor.

It was dark in the Hooch, both day and night. This was hard not only on our eyes but also on our spirits, and it caused a problem in terms of human sanitation. The North Koreans had made no provisions for latrines, so this became an immediate need. Our solution was simple: each day we dug a hole around the perimeter of our mud prison and placed two loose shards of wood we pulled from the center beams on either side of the hole. In theory, a soldier would locate the position of the wood, hold onto them, place his feet in the right position, and lean against the wall for support. In practice, it was usually hit and miss.

The North Korean farm boys were not the sharpest bunch when it came to holding prisoners. Each day they threw hemp rice sacks into the Hooch, not realizing these sacks would become a tool for our salvation. The sacks were tied on each side with string. We saved the string, slept on some of the hemp bags, and covered up with others for warmth. We stored the sacks above the rafters of the Hooch. Our supply of bags grew as each day passed, and we believed the North Koreans never had a clue we were using them for warmth. Although our conditions were still miserable, those rice bags gave us some hope in that dark and evil confinement.

Using the rice sacks for beds and blankets, we found that sleeping side by side in a large circle was the best way to share warmth and survive the extremely cold nights. Of course, the big problem came when someone had to get up in the middle of the night to use the latrine. One man's visit caused every other man to wake up and move. Eventually—and unfortunately—the guys relieved themselves in their pants. It made little difference anyway, because there wasn't any toilet paper, there was nowhere to wash our hands, and hitting the hole was merely by chance. It didn't take long before the Hooch smelled like an open sewer.

As a soldier, I had been trained in the importance of good sanitation. In Ranger school, I had been drilled in the importance of a clean shave, even if it had to be a dry one. But this was impossible in the Hooch, as we were never given water to drink, much less to use to clean up. All of us were in the same miserable condition. Early in our ordeal some of the men began bleeding rectally; by the end, all of us were. If it weren't for the moisture content in the watery slop they fed us, we would have been in even worse shape.

Because temperatures were fifty degrees below zero at the time of our capture, most of us were dressed appropriately for the weather. Except for those early tattoo checks, none of us ever took any of our clothes off during our imprisonment. We kept our hats with ear flaps and parka hoods on our heads and our rifle mittens on our hands. Everyone grew a beard within the first few weeks, so the only body parts you could see on a fellow inmate were his lips and eyes.

Being bundled up so severely against the cold reduced the amount of interaction and discussion we had with one another. Because of the nature of that final battle, the way in which our units had been scattered, and the lack of communication, the thirty-seven men in the Hooch were all from different units that had been in the general area. A few of our compatriots were even from the French forces. Although it may seem odd considering the close proximity we shared with one another, we didn't even know each other's names or what one another looked like. We saw daylight only when we were taken outside for roll call or to be beaten, and occasionally on a sunny day when the sunshine slipped through the cracks in the Hooch.

CHAPTER 10

TORTURE IN THE HOOCH

I N JANUARY 1954, the US Senate Committee on Government Operations, chaired by Senator Joseph McCarthy, published their findings on Korean War atrocities. The introduction to their report reads:

> On June 25, 1950, the North Korean Peoples' Army, without warning, attacked the Free Republic of South Korea. During the ensuing three years of warfare, the Communist enemy committed a series of war crimes against American and United Nations personnel which constituted one of the most heinous and barbaric epochs of recorded history.

Indeed, the beatings we suffered at the hands of the North Koreans were heinous and barbaric. Our guards knew nothing about the Geneva Convention or the humane treatment of prisoners of war. They only knew we were the enemy, and they had been charged with torturing us.

As if to make a sort of routine or to mark time, the guards began a schedule of daily beatings. I don't know why these daily beatings began—the North Koreans weren't seeking to beat information out of us. They didn't have the language skills to ask us any questions and even if they did, as foot soldiers, the men in the Hooch probably couldn't have supplied them with any crucial information. As I said before, it seemed as if the guards made up the rules as they went along. I could not understand why they kept taking us outside for beatings unless they felt some "moral" or fatherland-type obligation to harm the enemy.

There were no officers in our group of prisoners, and over time, I became our de facto leader. I think it was my Ranger training that made me keep an eye on the rest of the troops in the Hooch. One of my primary concerns was for the other soldiers' feet. The North Koreans, having small feet, had taken the boots from the prisoners who also had small feet. (Luckily, with my size twelves, I had no fear of my boots being taken.) To protect the feet of the soldiers who now were without boots, we wrapped their feet in rice sacks and tied them on with the string we had saved. These soldiers still suffered frostbite on their toes, but the sacks helped to keep their feet intact.

In addition to watching over the physical needs of the soldiers, I also felt compelled to care for their mental conditions. The routine beatings made this task difficult. It was hard to help a man deal with the mental and emotional agony of a beating on top of the agony of capture. This was especially difficult when the beatings took on a personal nature. Some of the guards were just cruel and liked to pick on certain soldiers in the Hooch, singling out those they saw as weak.

Compounding the problem were the "camp girls." I don't know where these girls came from, but they took extreme pleasure in kicking us in the groin. Fortunately, I was able to teach the guys how to lessen the blow. I instructed each man that as the guards held his head down, he should be able to see the kick coming. Just before that nasty foot hit, he should scream and squeeze his thighs together as best he could. By doing so, the direct hit would be less painful. Sadly, this technique was not as effective for the poor guys with skinny upper legs, but even in their agony I could sense they appreciated my leadership. All the men in the Hooch were looking for some sort of direction and wanted to know someone was looking out for them. I was that person.

The American units didn't have females around in those days, with the exception of the nurses in the MASH units, so the presence of these camp girls puzzled me. Eventually, I came to understand these girls were responsible for cooking and cleaning for the North Koreans—and they were also there for conjugal relations. This represented a major difference between the American forces and the North Korean Army. American soldiers were hound dogs with their noses to the ground looking for females anywhere and at any time, while the North Korean Army supplied their troops with women for that pleasure. Although it may have sounded like a great deal for the North Koreans, these women were cruel and likely riddled with disease.

I first noticed the camp girls during our sixth week of captivity. North Korean troops had descended on the camp, probably for food and rest. I heard loud talk, laughter, and excitement and knew something big was going on outside. That night, the guards who came on duty seemed intoxicated and in need of a place to sleep, and the guard shack outside the door of the Hooch was the perfect place. I believe about ten women serviced the entire group of North Koreans, which I guessed to be about 120 men. Although I tried to observe the patterns of the camp girls and soldiers, I could never figure out how the North Koreans decided which soldiers got to use the camp girls first, whether they drew straws, cast lots, or lined up by rank. The camp girls remained a puzzle to me, but I knew they were an important part of camp life, and continued to watch them carefully when I could.

Time passed, yet we had no way to mark its passing. There was no place to make a mark on the walls, and even if there was, there was barely any light to be able to see a mark. Our only time telling came in the form of quick comments between the Hooch men. "I think today might be my birthday." "Do you think it's almost Christmas?" I tried to keep track of the days in my mind, each day telling myself how many days I had been in captivity.

During our ninth week, the girls returned and the pattern continued: sex, liquor, excitement, and intoxication. At this point, a bright light went off in my head, and I wondered whether we could use the situation to our advantage. About ten of the men had started talking about making a plan for an escape. Nothing physically had changed in the Hooch. Conditions remained miserable, the beatings continued, the food remained abysmal, and the temperatures were still frigid—but there was a new sense of revitalization. Something *could* happen.

Although some of the prisoners were afraid of failure and did not want to talk about escape, most of us were behind the genesis of such a plan. I knew something had to happen. And soon. Some of the younger guys were becoming fearful of their next beating. About six of the men were really stressed, and I knew I had to do something to help them survive. When the guards entered the Hooch to select the soldiers to be beaten that day, we would try to hide the weaker men within our pack and surround them with the more able-bodied. However, the guards knew us by our hats and headgear, and would search through the pack for the men they knew would suffer most. If the guards grabbed one of those six for a beating, I would have to intervene with some sort of disturbance—pushing, yelling, bullying the guards—and make the guard so mad he dropped the poor soldier and grabbed the troublemaker—me.

In case you think I am some sort of Rambo, let me tell you that I was scared to death. Sometimes I threw up during a beating, and I always closed my eyes until it was over. I was never one who liked to be singled out, but I knew this was necessary if all thirty-seven of us were to survive. This was my way to help each man escape, as we all needed to be as physically and mentally strong as we could be. In war, being scared to death was a daily affair. If any soldier ever suggested that he had no fear in battle, I would suggest he had never been tested in those kinds of conditions.

My own testing intensified every day. Instead of a Rambo, I guess you could say I made myself into a rag. I was filthy, but I continued to allow myself to be used by my captors. Like a rag, I gave no resistance to the beatings. Like a rag, I was tossed back into the dark to be used another day.

Sometimes the guards slapped me in the face when they entered the Hooch. Often my nose bled, and because I had nothing to wipe it with, the blood dried on my face. The guards always took off my headgear (the hood of my parka or hat with ear flaps), which allowed them to grab the hair on the back of my head and make me bend over in a submissive position.

One day as the guards dragged me out of the Hooch by my long, dirty hair, they decided to take off my boots and beat my feet. I think they struck my feet twenty or twenty-five times with a bamboo stick. The beatings hurt so bad that I lost my breath and fell over. This made the guards angry, and they made me stand and walk back into the Hooch. The pain was so intense that I couldn't speak for several hours. Although the swelling went down in a day or so, I carry the memories and the pain of that beating to this day. I wish I could rip the memory out of my head, but even with shoes on I can still feel the pain if I simply step on something as small as a matchstick.

Despite the torture, I continued to be a thorn in the side of the North Koreans by causing a ruckus and drawing attention to myself, and they continued to make me pay. One day, I realized that maybe I had pushed them a little too far, and that they had no qualms about killing me. The guards had found a five-gallon can labeled in English. I could tell by their glee and elaborate gestures indicating explosions and fire that they thought they had found a can of napalm. Although I had never seen or used napalm, I had been educated on its use in Ranger training. Napalm was used by US forces in Korea to swiftly burn buildings, but became a household word in America during the Vietnam War, when the jellified gasoline was used as an anti-personnel weapon. These North Koreans were apparently ahead of their time. After tying me to a post in the Hooch, they fiendishly snickered and chatted back and forth as they covered me with the substance.

When the four guards were satisfied I was well covered, three of them ran for the door. The fourth was to light the "napalm." He was carrying a lantern and a long stick, which he lit to ignite the jelly and me. The stick burned slowly—not in a flash fire as they had expected. The last guard left the Hooch, dejected, and I could hear him complaining to the other guards outside, probably cursing the US and our lousy products. But from where I was tied to the post, I could read the label on the can: grease. Good old American crankcase grease. While the grease did burn and leave me with scars, it clearly did not have the intended outcome the guards wanted. The men in the Hooch soon put out the fire and helped me off the post. If the can had held napalm, my flesh would have been burned down to the bone, and everyone in the Hooch probably would have perished as the fire spread up the pillar to the hemp roof.

Throughout my ordeal, I never prayed (mostly because I didn't know how to do so) or asked God to get me out of the situation. Although I believed in a higher power, I was never a particularly religious person. The experiences of my early childhood had tarnished the word "religion" in my mind, and I had watched as my parents' religion drove a deep and painful wedge between us. Instead, I depended on myself, my gut, and my training to get through this ordeal.

I did, however, promise myself that if and when I got back to civilization, I would do something good every day—something kind or considerate for someone. I don't know where this idea came from, as I hadn't exactly had many examples of kind and considerate behavior in my life. I guess those few moments of kindness from Helen, Aunt Mary, Aunt Bell, and Uncle Dell had made an impression on me.

The 1954 Senate Committee on Government Operations concluded the following about the atrocities conducted against the American POWs in Korea:

Upon hearing the testimony of all witnesses and studying the documentary evidence submitted, the subcommittee advises:

1. The North Korean and Chinese Communist armies were guilty of the following war crimes and crimes against humanity committed against American personnel during the conflict in Korea from June 25, 1950, until July 27, 1953:

   a. Murder;
   b. Attempted murder;
   c. Malicious and aggravated assaults;
   d. Various acts of torture, i.e., perforating flesh of prisoners with heated bamboo spears, burning prisoners with lighted cigarettes and inserting a can opener into a prisoner's open wound;
   e. Starvation;
   f. Deliberate policy of fostering starvation;
   g. Experimental medical operations;
   h. Coerced Communist indoctrination;
   i. Bayoneting.

2. The Communist government in China is equally responsible and guilty as the Communist government in Korea for war atrocities committed against Americans.

3. Virtually every provision of the Geneva Convention governing the treatment of war

prisoners was purposely violated or ignored by the North Korean and Chinese forces.

4. *More than 5,000 American prisoners of war died because of Communist war atrocities and more than a thousand who survived were victims of war crimes.*

With the exception of the experimental medical operations and coerced Communist indoctrination, all these atrocities took place in the darkness and degradation of the Hooch. Senator McCarthy didn't interview me, but I would have told him the same stories that hundreds of other POWs shared at the hearings. What I would have *liked* to have told him is that I survived.

CHAPTER 11
ESCAPE

AFTER THE TWELFTH week had passed (with a few more beatings), the pattern of the North Koreans became clear to me: the women and booze came in every three weeks. When this time of North Korean-sponsored "fun" arrived in camp, the guards fell into their intoxicated and lusty states, and we would have an opportunity to flee.

We decided to make our escape during the "party" in the eighteenth week. The plan was for us to overpower the guards in the dark of night, leave the area as quickly as possible, and seek out friendly forces. This was as far as the plan ever progressed, as we had no idea where we were or where those friendly forces might be located. The idea of having an escape plan in place helped us get through each miserable day until that eighteenth week arrived.

Our excitement level mounted, but there was nothing we could do but wait. We continued to listen carefully and watch when we could catch a glimpse of the outside world. When the fifteenth week arrived, the routine was the same: women, liquor, intoxication, poor guarding. We counted down the days to the eighteenth week. Then, suddenly, our plan was put into jeopardy when the camp girls arrived on the seventeenth week.

We weren't sure if the girls arrived because of a Korean holiday or from a snap decision by the North Korean brass. Regardless, we had no time to ponder why the pattern had been broken. There was no time for us to worry or make new plans—we had to immediately leave, despite the fact there was more than sixteen inches of snow on the ground, which we had watched accumulate when we had been taken out for our daily beatings.

Even though we had been taken by surprise, we were ready. I was ready. We all understood the consequences if our escape plan failed. We would either be sent to a prison camp further into North Korea—most likely for execution—or we would be shot by the Hooch guards. During my days as an FO, I had been in many dangerous situations in Korea, but this was truly a do-or-die moment. We would either escape or die trying.

Many of the men were nervous, but most were more than ready to see our plan come to fruition.

When darkness approached, we knew the late guard shift occurred in about five hours. I talked to the men about our plan and stressed that failure was not an option. We knew that in spite of all the "fun" happening in the camp, guards were stationed at both entrances to the Hooch, and both would have to be "immobilized."

As we finalized our escape plan, some of the guys said to me, "You do it, Sarge." How easy it was for them to say, "You do it." But I had known this responsibility would fall on my shoulders. I was a Ranger, and long ago I had assumed the leadership role for this bunch of guys. They were depending on me to do what had to be done, and I knew I had the strength to do it. I was much weaker than I had been seventeen weeks earlier, but I was still among the strongest of the men.

We decided the thirty-six men would silently exit the Hooch on my signal after both guards had been taken down. The strongest men were assigned to lead the way, followed by the weaker men. When we felt the time was right, the men formed into their "escape formation," and I called out to get the first guard's attention. I knew I would have the element of surprise in my favor. None of the prisoners had ever resisted their captors for fear of being shot, so the guards had no reason to believe they were in any danger.

When the guard came through the doorway, I grabbed him from behind and covered his mouth, chin, and nose with my right hand. I slammed him back and down as quickly and silently as possible so the middle of his back fell onto my bent left leg. The fall caused the air to expel from his lungs, and I held him in that position until he became completely limp. There was no time for regrets or emotion. I did the same thing to the second guard, calling him into the Hooch and taking him down in the same manner. This is what I had been trained to do—to protect myself and the men under my lead by whatever means necessary. This was my mission, and I knew that for us to escape, I had no alternative but to kill the guards. Little did I know how much that necessary action would affect me the rest of my life.

Without talking or making any noise, we began our journey through the deep snow. The thirty-six men exited the Hooch just as we had planned and moved out as quickly as possible. I was the last one to leave, and I closed the doors behind me so everything looked normal from the outside. We knew we had at least four or five hours before the change of guard at dawn, and we pushed each other to get as far away as possible.

The night was clear and we moved well in spite of the snow. Although we were malnourished, our routine of calisthenics paid off, as we were able to make good progress even though many of the men were trudging through the snow in sack-covered feet. There was no looking back. The guards were not following us, and none of us had any longing for a last look. We focused on our forward movement.

At dawn we heard the sound of an airplane engine and saw a Cessna L-19 making wide circles in the sky. The US Army used L-19s (or Bird Dogs, as they were called) to watch enemy ground activity and spot artillery. The pilot dipped a wing to signal that he had spotted us. I could only wonder what he thought of seeing this long, caterpillar-like line of men trudging through the snow. He made another circle above us and gave us a directional flyover. He must have radioed in our position, for about an hour later we were met by a squad of soldiers who escorted us behind friendly lines.

When I was about forty yards from safety, I stopped and dropped to my knees. I was exhausted, relieved, and thankful we were almost free, but I was now overcome by a black cloud of guilt. As I thought of what I had done to assure that these thirty-six soldiers got home to their families, my mind's eye went back to the Hooch and those two young boys lying motionless on the floor. All of my fellow soldiers were now safe and taking their first steps back home, but all I could think of were the parents of those two young North Korean guards, parents who would probably never know where their boys were or how they had died.

That thought still weighs heavily on me every day. I have been told again and again that what I did was just an act of war—that it was part of the conflict and had to happen—but I think to myself, "That is easy for you to say." I wish those who were trying to comfort me could take one small glimpse through my eyes and understand the agony I have suffered because of that "justified" wartime action.

Of course, in my despair, my mind also travelled across the seas to my home in Chicago. I came to the miserable realization that if I had been the one killed inside the Hooch, no one would probably have shed any tears for me.

Cessna L-19 Bird Dog.

CHAPTER 12
RETURN TO LIFE

WHEN WE TRUDGED into the camp, most of the men collapsed onto the ground. We were quite a sight, and the commanding officer knew from our appearance that we were in bad shape. He came to me and said, "Soldier, let's get squared away." I obeyed his orders, got up, and followed him to a waiting vehicle. What I didn't know at the time was that the others had told him I was the leader of the group, the one who made the decisions, and the one who had killed the guards.

As we walked away, I looked around and saw that most of the men were being helped to the shower units or to the medics. I never saw them again. Of course, even after the men were cleaned up, we probably wouldn't have recognized each other. For weeks we had been disguised behind hats, parkas, dirt, thick beards, and matted hair.

The commanding officer took me to get cleaned up as well. I was such a mess that even washing hurt. They cut my matted hair from my head, trimmed away most of my beard, and I gave myself the most painful shave of my life. There was no warm water at the camp—that was available six miles away at a shower unit, which was merely a big tent alongside a body of water—and the cold water made matters much more difficult. It took quite a while to clean off seventeen weeks of dirt, filth, and hair, but when the crud finally came off, what a feeling of humanity. I felt like a new man.

The officers looked at my tattoo and said, "That has to come off." Although I had never had a tattoo before (much less had one removed), I knew the process was bound to be painful. My first thought: Why? Finally, someone explained that if I were captured again, my captors would see the tattoo and know I had been a prisoner before. They would probably execute me for that reason. All I could think at that point was: I guess I'm not going home. Wherever home was.

I had to wait for my skin to completely dry before they could begin removing the tattoo. Two days later, they took me to a MASH unit where the medical personnel literally sanded the skin off my shoulder. After what seemed like hours, they finally got to the ink and extracted the major portion of it. When a few days had passed I could see the redness from the rubbing, but not the number 31. I was glad to be rid of the tattoo, but I knew I could never be rid of the memories of the North Koreans who had put it there in the first place.

The army understood that I needed to get my head on straight, so they gave me five days of R&R in Tokyo. I stayed in a government-run hotel and was given the freedom to do anything I wanted. R&R was army-speak for "rest and recuperation," but a lot of the guys called it I&I—"intercourse and intoxication." My choice was to rest and recuperate, because after all I had been through I surely did not want to come down with a venereal disease on top of everything else.

During my time in Tokyo, I put to good use the one piece of advice my father had given me. One night, about midnight, when I was in downtown Tokyo, a girl came up to me and said, "Hi, GI, you come with me. I will give you a bath. We can dance." With curfew minutes away, I told the girl I had to go to the hotel and get my stuff. She rode in a cab with me to the hotel, and then I went in and never came back out. The next night I was downtown again, and that same girl saw me. She called me every bad American word she had picked up.

I remember one good soldier who went on his scheduled R&R and came back with what he thought was an incurable sexually transmitted disease. It troubled him so deeply that he took a Browning automatic rifle and ended his own life by storming an enemy-held hill all alone. Although not technically suicide, his death was assured by his actions. His action assured release from the humiliation of taking that disease home and being forced to explain his actions to a loved one. I think a medicinal cure was available, but he could not accept that he had placed himself in such a miserable situation.

It seems hard to believe, but the army considered those five days of R&R sufficient "therapy" for me to deal with my seventeen weeks as a POW/MIA. I was never ordered to see a psychiatrist, psychologist, or even a counselor. Command must have believed that five days in a hotel room in Tokyo should set me straight and relieve the trauma I had experienced. In the years since, I have heard much about post-traumatic stress disorder and the importance of diagnosis and treatment. I was never treated for this disorder, but in looking back I am sure I suffered from it. According to Dr. Robert Ursano and Dr. James Rundell of the US Air Force:

> *Post-traumatic stress disorder, depression, psycho-active substance abuse, somatopsychic disorders, and psychiatric disorders due to captivity-induced medical problems are all seen in returned POWs.*

The coexistence of two or more of these is the rule. Which is primary or secondary is usually less important than identifying and treating each. Individual psychotherapy (short- and long-term), family therapy, pharmacotherapy, and medical treatment for other diseases and injuries that may have resulted from captivity are all important parts of the medical treatment and follow-up of the former prisoner of war.[1]

When the Army Post Office finally caught up with me after all those weeks of my captivity, I only had six pieces of mail: two letters from the bank, two letters from Helen (the kind woman from my childhood), and two letters from Doris Colby, my so-called girlfriend. That's right, I said "girlfriend." We had met in Chicago after my father dialed her number, handed me the phone, and told me to ask her out. Doris and her family were members of my parents' church, and I suspect they hoped our date would draw me into the fold.

Doris was a nice girl, but not the drop-dead gorgeous sort I had envisioned myself dating. We had gone out a few times—once every three weeks or so—but she didn't play a significant role in my pre-war life. Consequently, I hadn't thought about

---

[1]Robert J. Ursano, MD and James R. Rundell, MD, *War Psychiatry* (Department of the Army, Office of the Surgeon General, Borden Institute, 1995), chapter 17, "The Prisoner of War."

her much during the entire time I was in Korea. Her second postmarked letter was basically a "Dear John" letter, informing me that because I hadn't written back after her first letter (which I couldn't have done because I was confined in the Hooch), she was now seeing someone else. Of course, there were no letters from my parents. I was not surprised, but again all I could think of was who would have accepted my corpse if I had died in North Korea.

I bided my time and was free of assigned duties as I awaited my new orders back into combat. Although I expected to be sent back to the front, much to my surprise, I learned the army was discharging me. Twenty days after my R&R was over, I was headed back to the States. My odyssey was now turning for the better, or so I hoped.

CHAPTER 13

HEARTBREAK

O N MOTHER'S DAY, 1952, I boarded another troop ship headed back to America, but this time I was in the relative luxury of a gunner's quarters. There were sheets on the cot and portholes I could look through to see the ocean. The best news of all was that I didn't get sick once on the return trip. I hoped the ship would make a stop in Hawaii so I could get a look at this gorgeous island chain and relax on a beach. Instead I found myself on the northern passage back to the States.

When I arrived in Washington State, I tried to call my parents to tell them I was safe and sound. There was no answer. Although I knew better, I made excuses for them—someone was sick, or they were at work or out of town. What a game I played with myself.

From Washington, I took the train to Illinois and then got on a bus headed to Fort Sheridan, north of Chicago. I settled in and was given leave at Fort Sheridan, and from there I took a train to the South Side of Chicago. I thought it would be fun to just walk up to my parents' place and surprise them. They would be so proud of me. After all, in the time since I had left, I had made sergeant, had been wounded and undergone surgery, had been held as a prisoner of war, and had been missing in action for seventeen weeks. What a great son they had.

Unfortunately, instead of a joyous reunion, I got the surprise. I knocked on the door of 1516 Marquette Road, but there was no reply. I waited, and then knocked again. I started knocking on all the doors of the apartment building in an attempt to locate my family. Finally, a lady on the second floor said she thought my family had moved. My parents had moved and changed phone numbers, and I had no idea how to find them. The woman told me to try 73rd and Maryland. I caught a cab to that address, and then sat on my duffle bag outside the building and waited for something to happen.

I waited and waited. After four hours, my mother and sister came around the corner at the end of the block. They saw me at a distance, but they didn't act surprised, happy, or relieved. There were no warm hugs or genial back-slapping. It was late spring in Chicago, but the coldness of my mother and sister made me feel as if I were back in Korea. How I had longed for a happy reunion. How disappointed I was.

Although I had never lived in this apartment, you could say that I had come "home" even though there were no pictures of me or mementos of my life with this family. During my second day there, after my father and sister had gone to work, my mother said she wanted to talk to me. We sat down, and she held out a letter that the Department of the Army had sent to the family. She looked it over as if she were reading it for the first time (which very well might have been the case) and asked, "What is this all about?"

I took the letter, scanned it quickly, and said, "This notice tells you that I was missing in action." Most mothers would have been shedding tears by this point, but mine only calmly asked, "Where were you?" So I told her about my experience as a prisoner of war and how I had been held with thirty-six other men by the North Koreans for seventeen weeks. There were no gasps or sobs, and she continued questioning me in an even tone.

"How did you get back here, then?" my mother asked.

"We escaped and made our way back to friendly forces," I replied. She asked for more details about how we had escaped, and although it was difficult, I explained that awful night when I had overpowered the guards and the group had walked through deep snow toward what we hoped were our own troops.

"What do you mean by you 'overpowered the guards'?" she said. I knew then that she and I were headed for a collision, but I decided to tell her the truth.

"We had to kill them," I said.

"Did you have any part in that?" she calmly asked.

"Yes," I confessed. "I had a major part."

She looked me straight in the eye and then, without emotion, said, "There is no room in this house for a killer. Pack up and get out." So I did. After all, what would have been the use in arguing with her? Despite the lack of motherly love, I knew this woman well, and knew that no amount of pleading or repentance would change her mind.

During the sixty years since this conversation took place, I have replayed that scene over in my head numerous times, always hoping for a different outcome. But, of course, it always ends with me leaving the apartment two hours later.

It might sound dramatic, but a lot of me died that day, especially when I found out that my mother had not shown the notification letter to my father or sister. I feared no one in my family had known or cared that I was missing in action, and I was right. No one would have claimed my body had we failed in our escape.

I got back to Fort Sheridan, dumped my duffle bag onto my bunk, and looked over the items from "home" that I had quickly shoved into the bag when I had been told to get out. There in the middle of my things was an item that made my heart sink even lower: a dime store flower pot with a fake flower. It had been a gift I bought for my mother when I was seven or eight years old, purchased with money I had earned on the streets. She had apparently tossed it into my duffle bag and in doing so, she sent a message loud and clear: our relationship, for what it was worth, was over. I was officially no longer a part of the family.

I don't have the words to express how traumatized I felt about this abandonment. If you lose a tooth, you understand the loss. If you lose an arm or leg, you can compensate. If you lose your mother because of death, your world stops. But if you lose your mother by her own choosing, the world not only stops but also becomes a dark and awful place.

As the day of my discharge drew near, I knew I would soon have to leave Fort Sheridan and the comfort of the army. This may seem like an odd sentiment to some, as one usually doesn't think of the army as comforting. "Army" implies a rough, tough, militaristic lifestyle. However, it had been in the army that I found fellowship and care, in spite of the traumatic experiences I had gone through.

The army put us soldiers first, making sure we were cared for and fed, which made me feel important. They did a tremendous job in getting supplies and necessities wherever we were located. For once in my life, it felt good to have such necessities given to me instead of having to scrabble for them myself.

I had learned important lessons in the army in addition to the skills I had been taught in Basic Training. I watched the Army Command move men and machines all over the Korean peninsula to where they were needed, which had been a great lesson in management. I also learned that while I might not agree with all the decisions management made, it was important to see the big picture and not make snap decisions based on what was going on in my little corner of the world. On any given day, we grumbled at Command's decisions, and then on another we marveled at its ability to see the future and get the job done.

I now faced the civilian world, where again I would be responsible for myself. I was still a young man who had been through a traumatic war, and now I had been abandoned by my family and left on my own. I didn't know where to go, so I called Helen, the woman who had looked after me when I was a little boy, and asked if I could stay with her for a while in Indiana. Much to my relief, she said yes. I never found out if Helen had known of my parents' decision to sever our relationship. I only knew that again, she had come to my rescue at one of the bleakest times in my life.

According to Drs. Ursano and Rundell, "*The family and the military community are critical elements in the recovery and readaptation of the POW.*"[2] My family didn't want me, and I had no inkling of where my life would take me next. But at least I had found a place to land for a while and a bit of the comfort I so deeply craved.

---

[2]Ibid.

CHAPTER 14
FINDING MY WAY

AS A BOY and a young man, I had always tried to be strong and brave in spite of what was going on around me—at least on the outside. Inside, I had been afraid most of my life. Growing up, my fear centered on the passive treatment I received from my family. Did they love me? Did they care for me? Would they let me die from injury or disease?

I didn't know, and it made me afraid. With each passing day, my fears about the disaffection of my family kept adding up one after the other. It reminded me of driving by telephone poles at a high rate of speed: each pole had meaning and purpose, but it was quickly passed by as something insignificant. The failure of one pole could mean the failure of the line as they all fell. Was my ever-growing pile of fears pointing toward my own failure?

I carried this fear into my teen years when I scrabbled for jobs and money. Although I tried to be a fun guy, my fears kept me in the shadows and made me lonely, even in a crowd. In the army, I suffered through some of the greatest fears a young man can face: combat, war, injury, capture, and the taking of life. I had been proven by example, tested under fire, and strong when I needed to be, but basically I was still a scared little boy looking for a little peace. I learned to seek out emotional hiding places and not come out until the coast was clear.

Now I was in Indiana with my bag and baggage, staying at the home of Helen, a woman I knew had some sort of love for me. I was twenty-four years old, and it was time for me to face another kind of fear: what to do with my life. I was afraid of failing, but at what, I didn't know. I was afraid of going into life alone. I was afraid I was a poor communicator and had ruined my relationship with my family. How many other relationships had I unknowingly sent into the ditch?

I knew I had to face these fears and try to carve out a life under Helen's protective wing. Helen and I weren't related, but I remember her as being one of the greatest supports in my life. She was the one who used to send me money for Kool-Aid when I was at the farm, and she was one of the few who wrote to me while I was in Korea. She was about ten years younger than my parents, but was kind and supportive to me in ways they never were. In fact, she treated me as the son she never had. Amen and thank you, God, for Helen!

Helen worked in an insurance agency that sold auto, fire, and general liability insurance. The office also had a growing business selling polio insurance, as that horrible disease was a huge concern to parents, who fearfully kept their young children away from movies, pools, and other public places. The owner asked if I might be interested in selling polio insurance door to door, so I studied for the insurance exam, took the test in Indianapolis, and started on my new career.

My own bout with polio should have made me sympathetic to the plight of these worried parents, but again I was trying to make a buck. I learned all the tricks of the insurance trade while I was in that job. When I spoke with concerned parents about the polio insurance, I always found a way to get them to tell me a little more information, and asked probing questions as to when their auto insurance was going to expire. I wrote down that information and passed it on to the other agents in my office, who called on those people when their insurance was about to expire. I was getting good at the insurance business, helping the company grow, and was soon making enough money for my living expenses.

My personal life seemed to be taking a good turn as well. When my "Dear John" girlfriend, Doris, found out that I had been captured by the North Koreans (and thus had a good reason for not writing back to her), she had an attitude adjustment. She wrote and said she was sorry about her misunderstanding and pitiful behavior. She was quite interested in reigniting our relationship, even though I was in Indiana and she was in Chicago.

Doris was not as indoctrinated in the faith as my parents were, and she was much more sympathetic to my plight and actions in the Hooch. But her mother and grandmother were staunch believers like my parents, and I didn't know how big of a fight I would have to take on for our relationship to continue. While I never went looking for a fight, I never ran from one, either.

In the middle of our renewed relationship, I was invited to go to a horse show with a gentleman whom I had known while I was in the horse business. The show was in Toledo, Ohio, and he was driving a harness horse. I was eager and excited to get back into the horse business, and I enjoyed the trip.

The man was vice president of a large meat-packing plant, and on the drive home he offered me a job. He told me I could start in the shipping department and work my way up into management. Things were really adding up—a job, a salary, and a girl. I asked Doris if she would be interested in marrying me, and she confirmed it was an option. So I took the position on the shipping dock and proposed to her. During our engagement we never talked about my parents, but there was always a little flicker of hope in my chest that because she and my parents were members of the same church, the marriage might be a bridge back to my family.

We took a five-day honeymoon trip to Florida, and to save money we stayed with her relatives along the way. Of course, we got the third degree night after night—the how, what, when, where, and why of our marriage. The shabby little apartment that waited for us back in Muncie, Indiana, looked better and better as compared to the nosey relatives we endured on our trip.

After we returned home, Doris got a job at a local bank. I was moved into management at the packing plant and continued to move up from job to job—first to the chemistry lab and then to assistant foreman in packaging, all within a six-month period. A few years later, I was promoted to general foreman of packaging and put in charge of scheduling production in the kitchen. By this time Doris and I had added two children to our family—one girl, Sharon, and one boy, Phil. We hadn't actually planned on having children, but I was quick to accept my responsibility, which increased tenfold since I was now responsible for finances, health care, and education for my children. Although I loved my children and considered them a blessing, I had no idea how to be a good dad, as I certainly had never had a good role model.

Always keeping my ears open for a good deal, I purchased property in the country, complete with a house, barn, some outbuildings, a pet cemetery, and surrounding acreage. It's possible I went a little crazy, but I filled the barn with chicken cages and then filled those cages with 2,500 egg-producing chickens. My children were growing up in the country, but they had a dad who went to work early in the morning and then came home after a long day to spend another four or five hours working in the chicken house. Work was (and is) an important part of my life, and I believed that if I kept myself busy and worked long hours, I could escape my past and the memories that haunted me. So I worked and worked, and never passed up an opportunity to take on more work. I didn't work myself to death, but I worked myself to skin and bones, weighing in at only 145 pounds soaking wet.

One day at the packing plant we had a visitor from Philadelphia who owned packing houses in the East. He looked at my operation, asked a lot of questions, and left. The next night he called me at home and offered me a job at the Philadelphia plant for more money than I ever realized existed. Doris and I talked and made a family decision that I would take the job and live at the company's apartment in New Jersey while my family stayed behind in Indiana.

The Philly plant was a union shop. I studied their production levels, but I was alarmed to find the plant used far too many shortcuts, which led to wasteful practices. I started to implement new ideas that not only saved the company money but also led to cleaner production and greater safety for the workers. The union, however, did not like my approach and started to fling idle threats my way. I was told to lighten up and play the game as it had always been played.

As I've said, I don't frighten easily, and the plant thrived under my leadership. The employees were happy, and my section moved into a $200,000 profit, a new high for that plant. Management was happy with me and made me the night superintendent. There was not much time for fun or sightseeing in this historic city of "brotherly love," as I was working twelve hours a day, six days a week.

I missed my family, and they eventually moved to New Jersey with me. The kids enjoyed the American Bandstand lifestyle of the early 1960s, and I started spending every spare moment with them. I knew I could do a better job than my parents had done, and I certainly didn't want my children to suffer the same fate as I had. Every Saturday I took the kids to breakfast and let Doris sleep in. On Sundays, the kids and I usually spent all day at the Jersey Shore or at other interesting places in Philadelphia or New Jersey. With my kids there, I could make time for fun.

But things were not so fun at the plant, as management continued to give me extra responsibilities and longer hours. My patience started to wear thin, and I knew something was amiss. Something just felt wrong—and it was. The plant owners were stealing from the federal government.

When a pig is slaughtered in a meat processing plant, the carcass is cooled and sent to a different department, where it is cut into pieces (two hams, two shoulders, four feet, fat back for lard, bacon, jowl, and so forth). The hams usually weigh from twelve to eighteen pounds each at this stage (this is called its "green weight"). At our plant, government employees purchased cured smoked hams for delivery to prisons and the armed forces. What the plant owners were doing was purposely adding brine to the meat to make the hams weigh two to three more pounds, so that when the buyer came back to check his order, the hams were back to green weight. If the buyer purchased a carload of hams, he was receiving hundreds of pounds of brine at the same price he paid for the meat, which was a dishonest practice.

I cannot say that I was always lily white, but I was never dishonest. Our plant had recently hired a new general manager and a new department manager, both from Indiana. They quickly realized that the plant was engaging in these dishonest practices, and they did not want to be associated with it either. We all wanted out.

When I drove to work each day, I passed a small plant full of Mister Softee trucks. Mister Softee was like a Dairy Queen on wheels. One day I stopped at the Mister Softee plant and struck up a conversation with one of the owners. He told me about some Mister Softee territories that were available, many of which were located in Indiana. I wasn't happy at my job, and I had no burning desire to remain in the East. The kids were getting close to school age, and Doris and I wanted to make sure they had the best education. So we talked about returning to Indiana.

I flew back to that state and found a house in Fort Wayne we could rent. After taking care of thousands of details, our family moved from New Jersey back to Indiana. I flew back to New Jersey one more time, and then drove a shiny new truck to Indiana. Guess what? I was a Mister Softee man.

As with every job I held, it was important for me to do the best I could, so I learned every aspect of the Mister Softee business. I drove the truck, made up the routes, sold ice cream, cleaned, and even repaired the truck when necessary.

One day, a builder in our neighborhood made me an offer I couldn't refuse. He had an open lot and said he would build us a home with a structure behind it that could house my trucks. Always looking for the next big thing, I said okay, bought two more Mister Softee trucks, and hired drivers for the routes.

My business was growing, and life was good. It was hard to believe that only fifteen years before I had been sitting in a cold, dark North Korean hooch, wondering if I would ever see "home" again. Now I was playing catch with my son and driving my daughter to music lessons and parties. I was lucky to be able to spend time each day doing things the kids liked. Although I was strict with my children and we had our ups and downs, as any family does, I was learning to be a good and loving dad. It was important to me that my kids knew me, trusted me, and relied on me for support.

At this point I purchased a 140-acre farm in an estate not far from where we lived. I walked into the bank and put $100 down to buy the place as is. There was no house on the property, but there was a barn and a few other outbuildings. The crops I sold enabled me to make the payments, and I bought my son a special horse. He loved that horse and wanted to pitch a tent out at the farm to stay with the animal. As much as I loved horses myself, I was the strict dad and made him come home.

The Mister Softee business was running well. When the trucks were off the road in the cold of the Indiana winters, I set my drivers up with work by opening Christmas tree lots for them to manage. Business was promising, so I thought about opening hard ice cream stores. With a little gumption and $12,000, I built my first ice cream store in a local shopping center. I named it Sally Sundae, which sounded to me like a happy little place people would like to gather and enjoy some ice cream. This, too, was a success, and after a while, to increase sales volume at the store, I added Spudnut donuts to the menu. Spudnuts were made from potato flour instead of wheat flour and were delicious.

One night approximately two years after the store had opened, the employee who came in early to make the donuts had a problem with the heat in the cooker. The oil boiled over the top of the deep fryer and began to burn. The fire department was called, and they called me, but when I got there the building was completely in flames. However, that was not my major concern. I searched, but couldn't find the woman who made the donuts. Luckily she had escaped, and I eventually found her, safe but a little scared.

When customers pulled up the next morning for their daily Spudnuts, all they saw were the charred ruins of my former business. I was heartbroken to see my ice cream parlor and donut shop devastated.

The next few weeks were a blur, but there was work to be done, so I got busy. I wrapped up the charred remains and remnants of this hope-filled business and tried to help my employees find new work. Then, it was time to re-focus my own career path.

CHAPTER 15

. . . .

NEW LIFE AND NEW OPPORTUNITIES

THEY SAY THAT when it rains it pours, so it was only logical that my marriage fell apart around this same time. The kids, who were now fifteen and thirteen, weren't getting along with their mother. I had long before been elected as the mediator and disciplinarian of our family, so it fell to me to handle the situation. The kids and I had a sit-down conversation with Doris, which turned into a debate and then into a full-blown argument. In the end, it was decided Doris would go live in Florida with her uncles for a while.

I was devastated about the approaching end of my marriage for all the usual reasons. We had built a life, homes, businesses, and a family together. Another finality hit me especially hard, though. I had hoped that my relationship with Doris could lead to a renewed relationship with my parents. That had never happened in the years we were married, and now probably never would.

Doris packed, took the best car, and headed for Florida. Meanwhile, I got my first taste of doing everything—of being both mother and father. However, I looked at this turn of events not as a hardship but as a challenge. As a single dad, I had the pleasure of getting to know my children better. Sharon was a studious homebody and a dependable young woman. Phil, on the other hand, was the athletic, wandering type. He loved horses, just like his old man.

After about two months in Florida, Doris called and told me that she was coming back to Indiana. She said that she had given the situation a lot of thought, and while she was not interested in raising the kids, she would keep the house, the dog, and all of her belongings. She also would keep her health insurance, which I was to pay for six months. I agreed and found a nice apartment in a golf-course complex for Sharon, Phil, and me. Although I was angry and frustrated with Doris, I made sure the kids visited their mother at least once a week. No matter what, she would always be their mother, even though I was now the sole caregiver, disciplinarian, and support for two teenagers. I don't know if raising my kids through their teenage years was a victory or a defeat, but I do know that it was a lot of work.

I have held a lot of jobs in my life, but I have to say parenting was the hardest, and it was even more difficult being a single parent. My goal was to raise children who would grow into honest, respectful, caring, and giving adults. I saw my new single-parent responsibilities as an opportunity for success. However, when dealing with two other humans who had two distinct personalities, success was not a sure thing but the result of trial and error. My kids, like all teenagers, needed to find their own way in the world—to "spread their wings" by seeking out their paths and becoming responsible citizens—and often during such journeys it fell to me as the parent to clean up the mess and control the situation.

For instance, one time, my daughter asked to spend a night with a girlfriend, which sounded like a fine idea to me. What I didn't know was that Sharon and her friend were planning to take a walk after dark with a couple of young boys. Unfortunately for her, I decided to take a different route home from work that evening and spotted her and her friends laughing and having a good time. When Sharon saw my car, she blinked at me like a deer in the headlights, and then she and her friends ran.

I slammed on the brakes and called out her name. Eventually, she came slinking out from between two houses, where the kids attempted to hide. Without a word, she got into the car. I didn't say a word either—I simply drove us home. Sharon went to her room, and she later said that she wished she could have just died that evening. It may have been harsh, but I grounded her for the rest of the summer.

As a teacher, Sharon now likes to tell her high school students that if they think *she* is tough, they should try living at *her* house with *her* dad. This tough old dad didn't even have to say a single word for her to understand that I was disappointed in her behavior. She knew what my expectations were and that she had let me down. The lesson must have sunk in well, because she has never let me down since.

Phil, my horse-loving boy, also made his share of mischief. One day when he was about sixteen years old, he decided that instead of going to school, he would go out to the farm to be with the horses. I'm sure he was having a glorious day atop his steed, thinking himself quite the sneaky rebel for ditching school—until his horse reared up and he fell off and broke his collarbone. He didn't feel so rebellious when he had to call me, confess his actions, and ask me to come retrieve him. We had a long talk on the way to the hospital.

After the disappointment of having the Sally Sundae/Spudnut store burn down, I felt as if I were adrift in a sea of responsibility. I wasn't in a panic, but I knew I had to make some money and make it quickly. Teenagers were expensive, and the bills were piling up. I wasn't sure if I should open another business, go back into the insurance or meat-packing industries, or find a completely different career.

Good fortune soon again came my way when a member of the Republican Central Committee stopped by my burned-out store. He had heard about the fire and the loss of my business, and he wanted to know what my plans were for the future. When I said I wasn't sure, he asked if I could meet with the Central Committee and listen to a proposition they had in mind. I was familiar with everyone on the committee, as I had served as a Republican precinct committeeman for a number of years. So I agreed, and a date was set for the meeting.

During the meeting, I was quizzed about my future plans. Honestly, I had none. The members of the committee asked if I would manage the largest license branch in the state, which was in Fort Wayne. At that time all positions in the Indiana license branches were patronage jobs and given to loyal members of the current ruling party as a "reward" for their service. I had been a loyal Republican all of my voting life, and listened to the committee's proposal carefully, thought about it, and finally said yes. At last I was beginning a new career.

My career challenge was met, but yet another loomed in front of me. During my children's early teen years, my eyesight started to get fuzzy. I went to an optometrist for a check-up, but he told me there was nothing wrong and that I should just expect bright light and outdoor sunlight to affect my vision. But my eyesight continued to get worse, so I went to see different optometrists in the hopes of getting a better diagnosis. One eye doctor suggested I wear see-

License Branch Manager, Fort Wayne, Indiana.

through bandages over my eyes, which meant I could not drive. I would have to walk or be driven, and being strong-willed, I decided I would walk. Because I could not see changes in elevations—such as curbs and sidewalks—I did a lot of tripping, falling, and embarrassing myself. But I knew how to win battles, so I walked on.

At the time, I had about twenty employees at the license branch. One woman on my staff named Edna Hilly told me of a doctor in Germany who was doing special research in the field of vision correction. Edna had come to America from Germany as a war bride and had remained in close contact with her family in Europe. Neither Edna nor I knew what was wrong with my vision, but we communicated with the German eye doctor.

The doctor agreed to take me on as a trial patient. After conducting extensive phone conversations (translated by Edna) and filling out a four-page questionnaire, the doctor sent a special medication to America for me to take. In two months my eyesight began to improve. A team of German scientists evaluated my questionnaire and the amount of medication I had been taking and determined that I was a victim of post-stress syndrome, which they believed had been brought on by my experiences in Korea.

The scientists' research was cutting-edge at the time, but of course, I didn't know it at the time, as no doctors or psychologists acknowledged the realities of post-traumatic stress disorder or the extreme symptoms it carried along with it. I knew I carried emotional battle scars. I knew other soldiers carried them as well, and many had succumbed to the horrors they carried in their minds by committing suicide. The German doctors advised me to continue the medication and try to ease my mind and relieve the guilt I carried about the events I never discussed. I did keep up with the medicine, but dealing with my emotions was another story. Eventually, my full eyesight did return, but I still carried the burden of my actions in Korea. I often wonder if the German researchers' investigation into my near-blindness was useful in treating other victims of post-traumatic stress. I surely hope others were helped by the results of my treatment.

The managerial job at the Fort Wayne license branch lasted about five years, and then I was "promoted" to the position of general manager for all three license branches in Allen County. During this same time period, a new Republican mayor, Robert Armstrong, was elected in Fort Wayne, and he asked me to also serve as his personnel and labor relations director. I took the personnel job, but from that time forward I refused pay for the license branch work, as that would have constituted a conflict of interest. Having two full-time jobs kept me busy, but by this time the kids were almost adults.

Armstrong lost his bid for reelection in 1978, and a Democrat took his place, which meant that my time working for the city of Fort Wayne was over for that election cycle. I went back to working just one full-time job at the license branches. During this same period, the governor of Indiana, Robert

Orr, was having some trouble with the State Bureau of Motor Vehicles (BMV), as positions within the Bureau had become highly political and the inefficiency of the Bureau was becoming embarrassing to the governor. Governor Orr would be known as the governor who reformed education, and he was determined to reform as many other Indiana government agencies as he could. He knew I was familiar with the ins and outs of license branch work, so he asked me to come to Indianapolis to help clean up the mess that came with twelve years of patronage and little oversight. I worked at that job for about six months.

One evening around seven-thirty, I was working at my desk when an assistant at the governor's office called and asked if I would come over to the capitol building for a meeting with Governor Orr. The state police had been informed that I was coming, and they were waiting for me when I arrived at the State Capitol. The police escorted me into the governor's office, and there Governor Orr asked if I had heard the rumors about the existing BMV commissioner. I told him honestly that I hadn't heard much, as the job of cleaning up messes within the BMV was taking up too much of my time, and I didn't really have time for office chit-chat.

Governor Orr said the commissioner had done some things to embarrass his office and he was going to make a change. Then he looked at me and said, "Are you ready for that big of a challenge? It will be happening very soon."

I said, "Yes, sir, I'm technically ready, but I would like to make some suggestions." The governor said to go ahead, so I made a list of the changes I wanted to see at the BMV: no more two-hour lunches, no drugs of any kind, no favoritism, and nepotism only for the opportunity to work and not for a lifetime job.

The governor agreed with my suggestions and said, "It's yours." Then he asked what my travel plans were for the next day. He told me that at 4:00 PM the next day—"not five till or five after"—he would be at the Bureau of Motor Vehicles offices to make the announcement. At 4:20 on that Friday, I became the new commissioner of the BMV.

My head was spinning that weekend, but I was not afraid to take the job. I knew more about the BMV than any other person who had held that position, as for years the governor's political "friends" had held the office without any previous knowledge of how the department functioned. This was a long-standing patronage system in Indiana politics which benefitted the winning politician's friends, but not necessarily the people of Indiana. Apart from overseeing the day-to-day activities of a major state bureau, the biggest job I faced was cleaning up the mess left by previous commissioners. I interviewed applicants for new department head positions, eliminated other positions, combined branches, and taught employees that their work was more important than just a political agenda. They were employees of the BMV Commission under the new law. After my tenure in the position, the Indiana BMV was in the black for the first time in seventy-five years.

My term ended in 1988 when a new Democrat governor was elected. I resigned, as I was expected to do, so that the new governor could place one of his own people in the position. The incoming governor, Evan Bayh, asked me to stay for four months during the transition, which I gladly did. I wanted to see all the accomplishments that I had made at the BMV continue.

Good fortune came my way again. Near the end of my four months, the mayor of Fort Wayne, Indiana's second-largest city, asked me to serve as the chairman of the Board of Public Works. The Board of Works was responsible for overseeing the street department, water and sewer departments, filtration plant, wastewater plant, and about 1,200 employees represented by seven unions. I accepted the position, worked for several years as chairman, and then retired in 1994.

Never one to sit around, I kept busy in my retirement. I started a small business sandblasting commemorative stones—family names, college logos, tee markers for golf courses, and headstones. After I sold that business, I designed and produced several inventions and became a master candy maker. I also give my time to the Meals on Wheels program in Hamilton County, Indiana, volunteering Monday through Friday. It fulfills a need in me and the promise I made years ago to help others.

I support the Wounded Warrior Project, which is a national organization that focuses on the needs of men and women wounded in battle. Although I would have been considered a Wounded Warrior, there were no programs like this available when I returned home from Korea. I feel it is my responsibility to aid in the housing, nutrition, and health care needs of today's veterans and to encourage and support them with both my time and my dollars.

I saw my mother very little after she asked me to leave her home in 1952. The last time we visited, she was living in a nursing home, and I took my children to see her. She didn't know who I was. She thought I was her brother. I don't know when my parents died or where they are buried, but I have since forgiven them. My sister had a successful career in Washington, D.C., married, and had a son. We are not close, but we do still communicate.

I wish I could tell you the stories of Helen and my dear Aunt Mary, the two women who truly cared for me as I was growing up. I didn't see Mary after my return from Korea—my separation from my parents also meant a separation from her and knowledge of her whereabouts and well-being. Likewise, I lost touch with Helen over the years and do not know what became of her.

CHAPTER 16

....

SEARCHING FOR MEANING

W HEN YOU WORK with a horse like the beautiful blind mare, you build a relationship. You learn to communicate with the horse in a way that she understands through soft words, gentle touch, and slow, careful movement. In turn, she learns she can trust you to lead her, care for her, and never harm her.

Everyone thinks he or she knows what "trust" means. One doesn't have to look it up in a dictionary to know this powerful word implies confidence, strength, and reliability. I have heard and used the word "trust" my entire life, but I have come to believe that neither I nor the dictionary can fully define this difficult human concept. Trust is difficult to acquire, a challenge to retain, crucial to preserve, and often necessary to renew.

I had realized at the early age of six that I was an unwanted child, and I was continuously aware of this fact my entire life. I was aware of the burden I was to my parents through episodes such as my father's verbal and physical expressions of exasperation as he tended to my wounded leg. And when I was moved to the back room though I was sick with polio, and when I was shipped off every summer to the farm. Again and again, my parents withheld their love and compassion from me. Their grave silence and distance spoke volumes to me and clearly indicated my place in the family. Most young boys can trust their parents for guidance and care. I could not.

Likewise, as a young working man, I quickly learned I couldn't always trust my co-workers. Competition for jobs, ranking, and salary created difficult situations that often led to a breakdown of trust.

The grim reality of my upbringing became a crutch I leaned on heavily during my eighty-three years. I used it as an excuse to not get too close to others and trust only in myself. Throughout my life, I became more and more dependent on these crutches. I dwelt in the past, thought constantly about the past, and used my past to defend my actions and explain my inadequacies. Loving others was difficult for me because I often reverted back to that lonely little boy who never felt loved, worthy, or wanted.

As I stated, I never asked God to get me out of the situation during my captivity in Korea. Although I believed in a higher power, I never developed a "trust" in God. Instead, I developed a powerful trust in my own abilities and my training to escape from the Hooch, knowing that failure would mean death. When that mission was a success, it placed another crutch under my spirit—the crutch of the guilt of using my bare hands to end two human lives. That crutch was further propped up when my mother kicked me out of the house and labeled me an unwelcome killer.

I had the strength to endure all the trials along my journey, but I was haunted by the cruel visions of my past. Although the memories were distasteful and unhealthy, I could never clear my mind of them, or my heart from that guilt. My actions, though necessary, weighed heavily on my soul, and I spent countless hours rewinding and replaying the final scenes of the escape again and again in my mind. I could never forget the young guards or their mourning families, the lives saved and the lives lost, the feelings of unworthiness and the nagging question of why I was spared.

I have always felt restrained by my past. But at this point in my life, as I have finally put pen to paper and shared these difficult stories, I have realized I need to dispel these crutches—these restraints—that have gained me nothing. The crutches of my past have never made me happy or helped me acquire a job or make friends, yet they continued to torment me. I have decided I do not want to go to my final resting place with my crutches in hand.

Looking back, I am somewhat ashamed to admit that I assumed I could deal with the experiences in my life—and the consequences—on my own. I thought I was strong enough to hold it all in and not burden others with my past. However, as I have made new friends—people of faith that I have learned to trust—they have encouraged me to tell my story. Through the pledge I made in the Hooch to use my life to care and do good for others, I am now surrounded by friends who have helped me to examine my life from a new and beautiful perspective. I know that I did not make this pledge to myself sixty years ago because of *where* I was, but because of *who* I am.

I am now prepared to make another pledge to myself and to those to whom I have given my trust. I pledge that I will open my heart and allow Christ the Savior to enter. In doing this, I know I can destroy the restraints of guilt that I have allowed to hold me captive for too long. I wish to be in harmony with the heart of God. I have been a part of some tough missions and know this may be the toughest one of all, but I also know it will be my most successful.

I am eighty-three years old at the time of this writing, and it is as if God is opening a new chapter in my life through the writing of these words. My journey—my odyssey—has brought me to this peaceful and joyous place. Perhaps God was just carefully plotting His time on target (TOT) for my life, so His power would land on me at the perfect moment.

Like the blind mare that trusted me, I will now place my trust blindly in the hands of my Lord. I will wait for Him. I will listen for His voice. I will come to know His voice when He speaks. And I will follow His voice, walk with Him without my crutches, and trust where He leads.

EPILOGUE

THROUGHOUT MY LIFE, I have been actively involved in service to others.

I have served my *country* in the United States Army.

I have served my *state* as commissioner of the Bureau of Motor Vehicles.

I have served my *county* on the Tax Review Board.

I have served my *city* as chairman of the Board of Public Works.

I have served my *community* as a Meals on Wheels volunteer.

I am blessed with good health and the ability to continue to serve others.

I am the father of two children, grandfather of four, and great-grandfather to one. I enjoy being kept up to date on everyone's activities via telephone or computer, as most of my family lives in different states than I do.

My future plans are to continue to serve wherever and whenever needed.

EPILOGUE

 National Personnel Records Center

Military Personnel Records, *9700 Page Avenue St. Louis, Missouri 63132-5100*

March 14, 2005

Mr. CHARLES LAYTON

RE:

Request Number: 1-315586805

Dear Sir:

The record needed to answer your inquiry is not in our files. If the record were here on July 12, 1973, it would have been in the area that suffered the most damage in the fire on that date and may have been destroyed. The fire destroyed the major portion of records of Army military personnel for the period 1912 through 1959, and records of Air Force personnel with surnames Hubbard through Z for the period 1947 through 1963. Fortunately, there are alternate records sources that often contain information which can be used to reconstruct service record data lost in the fire; **however, complete personnel/medical records cannot be reconstructed.**

The DD Form 214, Report of Separation can not be reconstructed.

By using the alternate sources available to this Center, NRPC employees can often reconstruct the veterans beginning and ending dates of active duty, the character of the service, rank while in service, time lost while on active duty and periods of hospitalization.

We are pleased to enclose NA Form 13038, *Certification of Military Service*. This document verifies military service and may be used for **any official purpose**. A seal has been affixed to this document to attest to its authenticity. The information used to prepare the enclosed NA Form 13038 was obtained from an alternate record source.

If you have questions or comments regarding this response, you may contact us at 314-801-0800 or by mail at the address shown in the letterhead above. If you contact us, please reference the Request Number listed above. If you are a veteran, or a deceased veteran's next of kin, please consider submitting your future requests online by visiting us at http://vetrecs.archives.gov.

Sincerely,

DELPHINE HOLMAN
Archives Technician (5A)

Enclosure(s)

National Archives and Records Administration
http://www.nara.gov/regional/stlouis.html

UNITED STATES OF AMERICA

Certification of
Military Service

****

This certifies that   Charles E Layton
                           55 043 640

was a member of the   Army of the United States

from   November 3, 1950

to   August 4, 1952

Service was terminated by   Honorable Release from Active Duty

Last Grade, Rank, or Rating   Sergeant

Active Service Dates   Same As Above

Date of Birth: N/A   Place of Birth: N/A

***************   *National Personnel Records Center*
Given at St. Louis, Missouri on March 12, 2005   *(Military Personnel Records)*
                                              National Archives and Records Administration

THE ARCHIVIST OF THE UNITED STATES IS THE PHYSICAL CUSTODIAN OF THIS PERSON'S MILITARY RECORD

This Certification of Military Service is issued in the absence of a copy of the actual Report of Separation or its equivalent. This document serves as verification of military service and may be used for any official purpose. Not valid without official seal.

NATIONAL ARCHIVES AND RECORDS ADMINISTRATION   NA FORM 13038 (REV. 04-01)

AFTERWORD

AS DIRECTOR OF volunteer services at Meals on Wheels, I have the pleasure of working with caring, kind, and compassionate individuals. Chuck Layton embodies these characteristics. His journey through life has taken him many different directions, but the theme throughout has always been to help others.

There have been many special moments with Chuck. As we delved into his past, I asked him to share his life experiences. He was sometimes reluctant, as he would have preferred to give facts instead of feelings, but I pressed on. I believe the hours we spent together writing the outline for his manuscript were therapeutic for him. I felt throughout the time we spent writing that God was at work in our lives.

Over time, my relationship with Chuck grew and he became part of my family. I was happy to share my faith with him and have him accompany me to church. We attended a Bible study together. Eventually, one evening he asked if I would lead him in the great confession of faith. Chuck was ready, at age eighty-three, to accept Christ as his Lord and Savior. We dropped to our knees. It was a special moment I'll forever cherish.

Chuck is one of my dearest friends and a great treasure in my life. I have learned much from him. He is a wealth of information, and he has lived his life in service to others. In addition to being a Korean War hero, he is now a brother in Christ and the most selfless man I know.

I have enjoyed every step of this journey in assisting Chuck with his memoirs. I fell in love with the little boy searching for a place to belong and with the soldier who so desperately wanted someone to see him off and welcome him home. My heart was touched as his story unfolded, and I am filled with pride that we have a published book to share with others.

My heart has been touched and my life has been blessed. To God be the honor and glory.

Tammy Elmore

It has been both an honor and a blessing to meet Chuck Layton and to have the opportunity to help him complete his memoirs.

My dear friend, Tammy Elmore, had often spoken of the wonderful man who delivered Meals on Wheels and who would enter her office every day with a bounce in his step, a smile on his face, and a good story to share. When the Meals on Wheels staff encouraged him to write his stories, Chuck at first resisted the idea, but finally sat with Tammy and told her of his life journey as she wrote down each word. Tammy was surprised, and Chuck probably surprised himself by sharing some of his most intense experiences, stories he had kept to himself.

One day at our monthly lunch gathering, Tammy told her group of friends that she and Chuck needed someone to help polish his story. Chuck hoped to share his experiences so others might find hope in his words. I made the off-hand comment that as an English major, I would be glad to take a look at the manuscript and see what I could do.

As the next year unfolded, Chuck's story began to unfold as well. With each meeting, I learned something new about this great man. One thing I learned was that he does not like to be thought of as "great." I was not allowed to use the word "hero" in his book, but I will use it here—Chuck Layton is an American hero. I am proud to know him, and proud to call him my friend.

Georgiann Coons
November 6, 2012, Chuck's eighty-fourth birthday

WinePressPublishing
Great Books, Defined.

To order additional copies of this book call:
1-877-421-READ (7323)
or please visit our website at
www.WinePressbooks.com

If you enjoyed this quality custom-published book,
drop by our website for more books and information.

www.winepresspublishing.com
"Your partner in custom publishing."